# PREFACE

In today's interconnected world, cyber threats are no longer confined to large corporations and government agencies. Small and medium-sized businesses (SMBs) have become increasingly attractive targets for cybercriminals, who recognize their vulnerability and potential for significant financial and reputational damage.

This book is designed to empower SMBs to navigate the complex and ever-evolving landscape of cybersecurity. It provides practical guidance and actionable strategies to protect sensitive data, mitigate risks, and build a robust cybersecurity posture.

Whether you're a seasoned business owner or just starting out, this book will equip you with the knowledge and tools you need to safeguard your business from cyberattacks. We will explore a range of topics, including:

- **Understanding the Cyber Threat Landscape:** We will delve into the tactics, techniques, and procedures used by cybercriminals, from phishing attacks to ransomware.
- **Building a Strong Cybersecurity Foundation:** We will discuss the essential components of a comprehensive cybersecurity program, including network security, endpoint security, and data protection.
- **Implementing Effective Security Measures:** We will provide practical tips and best practices for implementing security controls, such as firewalls, intrusion detection systems, and user access controls.
- **Responding to Cyberattacks:** We will cover incident

response planning, including steps to take in the event of a cyberattack, such as containment, eradication, and recovery.

- **Staying Ahead of the Curve:** We will explore emerging threats and trends in cybersecurity, and discuss how to stay informed and adapt to the evolving landscape.

By following the guidance provided in this book, SMBs can significantly reduce their risk of cyberattacks, protect their valuable data, and maintain their business continuity. Let's embark on this journey together and secure your digital future.

# CYBER SECURITY IN THE SMALL AND MEDIUM BUSINESS

# INDEX

# 1.1 INTRODUCTION OF WHAT IS CYBER SECURITY

When we talk about cybersecurity we include all of procedures putted in place to protect systems, networks and programs from cyber-attacks. The main objective of a cyber-attacks are to get access, to change or destroy personal data. What do you mean for personal data? Personal data is any information that allows us to identify an individual such as: name, address, telephone number, email, medical conditions, training records, shopping preferences, location data and online behaviour. Once the hackers will get access to these personal data they could do whatever they want with it such as selling them to the best offer, extorting the owner to get it back in exchange of money or even interrupt the full business process. Every day is getting more complicated to implement an effective cyber security for many reasons, first of all the technology is developing and changing constantly and also because there isn`t yet a full awareness of the problem and possible impacts of losing data in the owners of personal data and in the business acquiring it.

Cyber security to be called effective needs to have multiple layers of protection distributed on all level of technology, protecting the hardware and software, protecting the cloud and network. We need also to make sure that all employee and all owners of personal data are aware of the important of their role in protecting those data, because every single of them play an essential role in the protection and implementation of an effective cyber security. Most of cyber-attacks still use the human factor to have a full access. These human factors usually lead to a data breach, most common are lack of awareness, negligence, or inappropriate access control. Human factors are not easy to mitigate, with the machine would be easier to identify and solve a problem, but you can`t fix a "faulty" employee in the same way that you fix a machine. There is always a reason why humans make errors. Our main objective is to understand why the errors were made and to find procedure to follow so we will avoid similar situations in the future.

A business after a cyber-attack could lose money, time and especially reputation, a costumer with a basic understanding of cyber security would never choose a business with a very poor reputation on data protection, Facebook in 2018 after the scandal on the inappropriate use of data lost 20% of users activity[1].

The authority, especially at European level, are making the foundations to a general ecosystem on the cyber security in all Europe. This foundations are based on the fact that cyber security is a share responsibility of everyone involved in it. Government, business, institutions and the users must take their responsibility to make our society safer, especially now with the increasing informatization of the world around us.

Cyber security, privacy legislation and GDPR (General Data Protection Regulation) are different pieces of the same puzzle that must be putted in the right to position to harmonize the new world that we are facing.

Small business owner, easily read the seemingly never-ending headlines about cybersecurity breaches at enterprise companies and be lulled into thinking that you aren't a target. After all, hackers are after the massive storehouses of customer data or proprietary information held by leading companies. While the biggest headline-grabbing hacks involve large companies, cybercriminals don't discriminate by size. As a matter of fact, even some of the biggest data breaches of the 21st century started out at small businesses. The cyberattacks that hit major retailer exposing the personal data of more than 100 million accounts, were carried out via the network small business. Two thirds of companies with fewer than 1,000 employees have experienced a cyberattack, and 58 percent have experienced a breach. These statistics make it clear all businesses need a solid cybersecurity strategy[2]. Be it ransomware, DDoS (distributed denial of service), phishing or some other threat, there is no shortage of cyberthreats targeted at small businesses. Hackers know that even small companies traffic in data that's easy to offload for a profit on the Dark Web such as medical records, credit card information, Social Security numbers, bank account credentials, and proprietary business information. Cybercriminals are always trying to come up with new ways to steal this data. They either use it themselves to get into bank accounts and make fraudulent purchases or sell it to other criminals who will use it. Sometimes cyberhackers are interested only in using a company's computers and conscripting them into an army of bots to perpetrate massive DDoS attacks. DDoS works by artificially generating enormous amounts of web traffic to disrupt service to a company or group of companies. The hijacked bots help generate the disruptive traffic. Today's businesses are digitally connected to each other to complete transactions, manage supply chains, and share information. Since larger companies presumably are tougher to penetrate, hackers target smaller partners as a way to get into the systems of large companies. Enterprise organizations have entire teams devoted to handling cybersecurity. At many small businesses, those efforts, if undertaken at all, are handled by someone who likely wears many other hats in the day-to-day operation of the business. That makes small businesses particularly vulnerable to hackers. To achieve peace of mind in the modern threat landscape, small business owners need to have a solid security strategy in place. That kind of preparedness starts with a solid understanding of the current threats, that will be explained more in deep in the next chapter but let`s have a general look at them[3]:

- Phishing: Often providing a gateway for ransomware or other infections, phishing typically works by goading users into clicking an email attachment or URL containing a virus. Phishing has become more and more sophisticated, and it can be incredibly difficult to spot a fake message as hackers target specific individuals with messages they can't resist.

- Ransomware: Hackers use a wide range of methods to target businesses, ransomware being one of the most common. Ransomware locks up computers and encrypts data, holding it hostage. For owners to regain access to their data, they have to pay ransom to a hacker who then releases a decryption key.

- Malvertising: Short for "malware advertising" this consists of delivering malware to a network after a user clicks on an apparently legitimate advertising. Identifying malvertising isn't easy because of the way it's disguised, but some advanced malware detection systems are getting better at it.

- Clickjacking: Similar to malvertising, this practice involves hiding hyperlinks to compromised webpages in legitimate website links. Users are then asked to reveal personal data that hackers steal for nefarious purposes.

- Drive-by downloads: This dirty trick downloads malware into networks, often without users realizing what is happening. Sometimes users have to respond to a pop-up window for the download to occur but other times all you have to do is unwittingly visit a compromised website.

- Software vulnerabilities: Hackers exploit vulnerabilities in popular web platforms like WordPress, tools like Java, and file formats, such as HTML, PDF, and CSV to deliver malware. Falling behind on updates can leave systems particularly vulnerable.

Any organization that neglects cybersecurity is taking a huge risk. And as businesses grow more and more interconnected, those risks extend to customers, partners, and suppliers. To ensure peace of mind and protect against costly malware, ransomware, and bots, small businesses need to implement 360-degree cybersecurity measures that include antivirus programs, firewalls, and network security solutions that proactively protect all devices connected.

One of the main event that shaped cybersecurity legislation around the world happen in 2018[4]. Facebook was the major actor involved in a security incident that exposed the account data of millions of users. Facebook says at least 50 million users' data were confirmed at risk after attackers exploited a vulnerability that allowed them access to personal data. The company also preventively secure 40 million additional accounts out of an abundance of caution. Facebook CEO Mark Zuckerberg said that the company has not seen any accounts compromised and improperly accessed. But Zuckerberg said that the attackers were using Facebook developer APIs to obtain some information, like "name, gender, and hometowns" that's linked to a user's profile page. Facebook said that it looks unlikely that private messages were accessed. No credit card information was taken in the breach, Facebook said. When a user enter username and password on most sites and apps, including Facebook, the browser or device is set an access tokens. This keeps the user logged in, without having to enter their credentials every time you log in. But the token doesn't store passwords, so there's no need to change password after this attack. Facebook says it reset the access tokens of all users affected. That means some 90 million users will have been logged out of their account, either on their phone or computer, in the couple of days after the attack. This also includes users on Facebook Messenger.

The vulnerability was introduced on the site in July 2017, but

Facebook didn't know about it until September 16, 2018, when it spotted a spike in unusual activity. That means the hackers could have had access to user data for a long time, as Facebook is not sure when the attack began. Facebook doesn't know who attacked the site. Facebook has in the past found evidence of Russia's attempts to meddle in American democracy and influence our elections but it's not to say that Russia is behind this new attack. Attribution is incredibly difficult and takes a lot of time and effort. It recently took the FBI more than two years to confirm that North Korea was behind the Sony hack in 2016. In July 2017, Facebook inadvertently introduced three vulnerabilities in its video uploader, said Guy Rosen, Facebook's vice president of product management, in a call with reporters. When using the "View As" feature to view your profile as someone else, the video uploader would occasionally appear when it shouldn't display at all. When it appeared, it generated an access token using the person who the profile page was being viewed as. If that token was obtained, an attacker could log into the account of the other person. Facebook says that the problem was fixed on September 27 of the same year, and then began resetting the access tokens of people to protect the security of their accounts. Facebook said that it's not yet sure if Instagram accounts are affected, but were automatically secured once Facebook access tokens were revoked. Affected Instagram users had to unlink and relink their Facebook accounts in Instagram in order to cross post to Facebook. On a call with reporters, Facebook said there is no impact on WhatsApp users at all. If an attacker obtained user Facebook access token, it not only gives them access to your Facebook account as if they were the user them self, but any other site that you've used Facebook to login with, like dating apps, games, or streaming services. If Facebook is found to have breached European data protection rules the company can face fines of up to four percent of its global revenue. However, that fine can't be levied until Facebook knows more about the nature of the breach and the risk to users. Another data breach of this scale, especially coming in the wake of the Cambridge Analytica scandal and other data leaks, has some in Congress calling for the social network to be regulated. Sen. Mark Warner (D-VA) issued a stern reprimand to Facebook over today's news, and again pushed his proposal for regulating companies holding large data sets as "information fiduciaries" with additional consequences for improper security. FTC Commissioner Rohit Chopra also tweeted that "I want answers" regarding the Facebook hack. It's reasonable to assume that there could be investigators in both the U.S. and Europe to figure out what happened.

Couple of time it was mention, previously in this text, the Cambridge Analytica scandal, let`s have now a look in what this scandal was about[5]. In March 2018, The New York Times, working with The Observer of London and The Guardian, obtained a cache of documents from inside Cambridge Analytica, the data firm principally owned by the right-wing donor Robert Mercer. The documents proved that the firm, where the former Trump aide Stephen K. Bannon was a board member, used data improperly obtained from Facebook to build voter profiles. The news put Cambridge under investigation and thrust Facebook into its biggest crisis ever. The Times reported that in 2014 contractors and employees of Cambridge Analytica, eager to sell psychological profiles of American voters to political campaigns, acquired the private Facebook data of tens of millions of users, the largest known leak in Facebook history until what happened couple of months after in September. The times article first showed how Cambridge received warnings from its own lawyer, Laurence Levy, as it employed European and Canadian citizens on campaigns, potentially violating American election law. The Times also found that tranches of raw data still existed beyond Facebook's control. In a companion piece, The Times reported that people at Cambridge Analytica and its British affiliate, the SCL Group, were in contact with executives from Lukoil, the Kremlin-linked oil giant, as Cambridge built its Facebook-derived profiles. Lukoil was interested in the ways data was used to target American voters, according to two former company insiders. SCL and Lukoil denied that the talks were political in nature and said the oil giant never became a client. The articles drew an instant response in Washington, where lawmakers demanded that Mark Zuckerberg, Facebook's chief executive, testify before Congress. Democrats looking into Russian interference in the 2016 election  already interested in Cambridge's role in providing analytics to the Trump campaign,— said they would seek an investigation into the leak. They were echoed by lawmakers in Britain investigating Cambridge Analytica's role in disinformation and the country's referendum to leave the European Union. The Times reported on a growing number of Facebook users, including the singer Cher, deleting their accounts — and broke news of the departure of Facebook's top security official, who had clashed with other executives on how to handling discontent over the platform's role in spreading disinformation. The hashtag #DeleteFacebook began trending on Twitter. After remaining silent for days, spurring another social media hashtag, #WheresZuck?, Mr. Zuckerberg spoke with The Times about steps Facebook was taking to address users' anger. As Facebook reeled, The Times delved into the relationship between Cambridge Analytica and John Bolton, the conservative hawk named national security adviser by President Trump. The Times broke the news that in 2014, Cambridge provided Mr. Bolton's "super PAC" with early versions of its Facebook-derived profiles, the technology's first large-scale use in an American election. The Times and The Observer reported allegations that the 2016 "Brexit" campaign used a Cambridge Analytica contractor to help skirt election spending limits. The story implicated two senior advisers to Prime Minister Theresa May. Testifying to Parliament a few days later, a former Cambridge employee, Christopher Wylie, contended that the company helped swing the results in favour of Britain's withdrawal from the European Union. The Silicon Valley spy contractor in another report, The Times showed how an employee at Palantir Technologies, an intelligence contractor founded by the Trump backer and tech investor Peter Thiel, helped Cambridge harvest Facebook data. The article reported that Palantir and Cambridge executives briefly considered a formal partnership to work on political campaigns. Though the deal fell through, a Palantir employee continued working with Cambridge to figure out how to obtain data for psychographic profiles. Palantir officials said the employee did so in a strictly personal capacity. The Times originally reported that Cambridge harvested data from over 50 million Facebook users. But at the bottom of a company announcement about new privacy features, Facebook's chief technology officer, Mike Schroepfer, issued a new estimate for the number of users who were affected: as many as 87 million, most of them in the United States. Amid the crisis, one set of voices remained notably absent: Facebook users whose data was harvested. So The Times found some, and their reactions ranged from anger to resigned annoyance at how tech giants use personal information. As one of the affected Facebook users put it, "You are the product on the internet." The Times also reported new details on the app used to collect data for Cambridge Analytica. It was no simple Facebook quiz, as many had assumed. Rather, it was attached to a lengthy psychology questionnaire hosted by Qualtrics, a company that manages online surveys. The first step for those filling out the questionnaire was to grant access to their Facebook profiles. Once they did, an app then harvested their data and that of their friends. Mr. Zuckerberg made his first appearance before Congress, testifying to Senate and House committees. First up was the Senate, where he faced tough questions about the company's mishandling of data, and said Facebook was investigating "tens of thousands of apps" to see what information they harvested. The next day, he faced an even tougher crowd in the House. There, the consensus was that social media technology and its potential for abuse , had far outpaced Washington, and that Congress may have to step in to close the gap. Even Mr. Zuckerberg seemed to suggest he could be open to some regulation, but neither he nor lawmakers seemed sure about how exactly to regulate the new breed of companies. On the same day as the Senate hearing, The Times reported how the Cambridge furore had impacted the Mercers, particularly Mr. Mercer's daughter Rebekah, who leads the family's political network. Shortly after the scandal broke, a friend of hers visited Facebook headquarters to plead the case for Cambridge. Though the Mercers were once Mr. Trump's leading patrons in conservative politics, their standing in the president's circle has suffered. The Times reported on a series of assessments of Facebook's privacy programs, conducted by the consulting firm PwC on behalf of federal regulators. In the assessments, mandated by a 2011 consent decree, PwC deemed Facebook's internal controls effective at protecting users' privacy, even after the social media giant lost control of a huge trove of user data that was improperly obtained by Cambridge Analytica.

Those 2 scandals should make everyone understand how important is to understand what are the critical part of the internet and what are the measure to have an effective cybersecurity culture at all levels, starting from the individual to the most important CEO of the biggest companies in the world.

# 1.2 WHAT ARE THE PRINCIPAL MEASURE IN CYBER SECURITY

As we mentioned already in the first paragraph cyber security to be effective need to work on different layers in the organization, in this paragraph we are going to see what are the principal measure and how they work[6].

-   Backing up the data. Data are always the main objective when it comes to cyber-attacks, as we said already the hacker when is attacking the main objective is to steal, destroy or change our data, or even worst blackmailing the owner of the data to get it back. For business especially that are in possession of their data plus the customer data is essential that they put in place all possible precaution to protect those from those attacks. Backing up the data is good not only to protect from cyber-attacks but also against incident that can happen because of a flood, fire or a software/hardware malfunction. The first important step in this procedure is to identify the essential data, what do we mean for essential data? All of those data that without the business could not function, usually consist of documents, photos, emails, contacts, and calendars stored on few devices as laptop, mobile phone, tablet, share drive or hard drive. The second action that should be taken into consideration when it comes to backing up the data is to save those data on a share drive/ pen drive and to keep it separate from the main device. Also the access should be restricted to less people as possible. A third action would be to consider a cloud storage service. The service provider will offer the user storage space and security of the files stored. Last step very important is to back up the data daily as loss, damage or cyber-attacks can happen at any times. So by backing up daily you will have access to the most recent data quickly.

- Protect your business from malware. A malware is a malicious software, in the form of a software or web content that hackers use to harm business. The most common malware is viruses. Viruses are self-copying programs that infect legitimate software. The best way to reduce and control attacks from the malware are many. First all should be installed and run an antivirus software. Another way is control what are the applications and programs installed into the devices, only approved by the administrator must be download. Next step would to keep all application up to date because also is part of the duty of the developer of applications and programs to keep them as safe as possible, with new patches the developer update the application or program in the safer possible version. A fourth step would be to control the access of external device such as USB drives and external and memory card. Is true that is one of the easiest way to pass data from a device to another but is enough one infected device to pass the virus from on device to another. So it would better to restrict the access to know device and have a specific antivirus in place to scan the USB device or the memory card before allowing the device to access. Last but not least it is necessary to switch on the firewall. The firewall build a wall between main network and the external network such as the internet. In this way is going to be easier to detect possible threats.

- Keeping the devices safe. Mobile and desktop device are the essential part in all business. Every user need to make sure to protect them as much as possible following these steps. All devices must be password protected with a suitably complex letter, number and character combination password. Many devices nowadays have the finger or facial recognition that make the device safer. All devices when lost or stolen they have to function to first of all locate them, if it is not possible to locate them is necessary to a feature to wipe remotely the memory so no one can access to it or to lock them permanently. Very important is also what we were saying before having a backup of the device memory so even though the device is stolen or lost we can have access to the last data in the back up files. Very important is to keep all devices and applications inside all up to date because as we were saying before the developer always release updates where there is the most secure version of the software. Last is very important not to connect to unknow WI-FI hotspots, such us public WI-FI, because someone else might have access to the data at the same time.

- 		Using password to protect your data. As we mention already using password to protect the date is one of the most important thing to do. Passwords, when implemented correctly, are a safe and free tool to prevent unauthorised access to personal data. On the portable electronic device the password could be subsite from a authentication method such as finger prints and facial recognition. On laptop device we have the standards letters, numbers combinations of digits to prevent untheorized access. The main objective when selecting a password is to make it as less personal as possible, so even for someone that know us would be difficult to guess and to make it complex a long enough to discourage any attempt to guess it, for example using a combination of numbers, letters and characters with a mix of upper and lower case. Very important is to change all default password and select a personalized one. last if there is the possibility to use a 2-step verification. A 2-step verification is adding a large amount of security to the device as is a combination of two protections to access, usually the password and another method, for example could be a code sent to another device that is needed to access the first device.

-       Avoiding phishing attacks. In a phishing attack the scammer send emails to thousands of people. In those email the receiver is trick to give sensitive information to the sender, or with a link to bad website. The reason why the sender is trying to do is to trick the receiver into sending money, steal details to sell on or the sender might have political or ideological motives for accessing organisation`s information. The main issue of phishing emails is that those email are getting harder to spot, even the most observant users could be tricked. There are several tactics to avoid or minimize this risk, for example configuring the accounts of staff using the principle of "least privilege". This concept is to give staff the lowest level of user right to perfume their jobs so if they are victim of phishing email the damage are reduced. Only who really needs should have  administrator privileges. The staff should be trained in recognised those kind of emails and understand what someone might target. There are some obvious signs of phishing, the staff should be trained in recognised that. Many scams originate overseas and often there are grammar and spelling mistakes. The scammer will try to create official-looking emails even including graphics and logo. As the scammer usually send the same message to thousands of accounts is not addressed directly to the receiver, the name of the receiver is not in the email or the name is wrong. Another sign could be that the scammer ask you to act urgently. Last but not least the sender email isn`t an official email from the enterprise that allegedly is sending the email, for example the email is signed by Amazon and the email is example@scammer.com.

In this paragraph briefly we describe some threats and measure to minimize them. In the following pages we will go back to them and adapt to different type of business. But now briefly let`s see what are the steps that a small size business can take to protect their cyber net as a small business, usually might feel helpless against cyberattacks. The following steps can be taken to protect companies by keeping up with the latest security ideas for businesses. Here are some essential business cybersecurity tips[7]:

- Train employees: Employees can leave business vulnerable to an attack. While precise statistics vary by country and industry sector, it is unquestionably the case that a high proportion of data breaches are caused by insiders who either maliciously or carelessly give cybercriminals access to your networks. There are many scenarios that could result in employee-initiated attacks. For instance, an employee might lose a work tablet or disclose login credentials. Employees may also mistakenly open fraudulent emails, which can deploy viruses on your business' network. To protect against threats from within, invest in cybersecurity training for employees. For example, teach staff the importance of using strong passwords and how to spot phishing emails. Establish clear policies describing how to handle and protect customer information and other vital data.

- Carry out risk assessment: Evaluate potential risks that might compromise the security of your company's networks, systems, and information. Identifying and analysing possible threats can help devise a plan to plug security gaps. As part of risk assessment, determine where and how data is stored and who has access to it. Identify who may want to access the data and how they may try to obtain it. If business data is stored in the cloud, is possible to ask the cloud storage provider to help with a risk assessment. Establish the risk levels of possible events and how breaches could potentially impact the company. Once this analysis is complete and have identified threats, the information collated must be used to develop or refine security strategy. Review and update this strategy at regular intervals and whenever there are changes to information storage and usage. This ensures data is always protected to the best of business ability.

- Deploy antivirus software: Choose antivirus software that can protect all devices from viruses, spyware, ransomware, and phishing scams. Make sure the software not only offers protection, but also technology that helps clean devices as needed and resets them to their pre-infected state. It's important to keep antivirus updated to stay safe from the latest cyber threats and patch any vulnerabilities.

- Keep software updated: As well as antivirus, all the software used to keep business running should be kept up-to-date. Vendors regularly update their software to strengthen it or add patches that close security vulnerabilities. Bear in mind that some software, such as a Wi-Fi router's firmware, may need to be manually updated. Without new security patches, a router – and the devices connected to it – remain vulnerable.

- Back up your files regularly: If a cyberattack happens, data could be compromised or deleted. Is important to consider the amount of data that may be stored on laptops and cell phones – without this, many businesses wouldn't be able to function. To help, make use of a backup program that automatically copies your files to storage. In the event of an attack, all files can be restored from backups. Choose a program that gives you the ability to schedule or automate the backup process so employee don't have to remember to do it. Is important to store copies of backups offline so they don't become encrypted or inaccessible if your system suffers a ransomware attack.

- Encrypt key information: If business deals with data relating to credit cards, bank accounts, and other sensitive information on a regular basis, it's good practice to have an encryption program in place. Encryption keeps data safe by altering information on the device into unreadable codes. Encryption is designed with a worst-case scenario in mind: even if data is stolen, it would be useless to the hacker as they wouldn't have the keys to decrypt the data and decipher the information. That's a sensible security precaution in a world where billions of records are exposed every year.

- Limit access to sensitive data: Within business, is essential to restrict the number of people with access to critical data to a minimum. This will minimize the impact of a data breach and reduce the possibility of bad faith actors from within the company gaining authorized access to data. A plan should be set up which outlines which individuals have access to certain levels of information, so that roles and accountability are clear to all involved.

- Secure Wi-Fi network: if business is using the WEP (Wired Equivalent Privacy) network, should be switched to WPA2 or more later, as these versions are more secure. It's likely that most business are using already WPA2 but some businesses neglect to upgrade their infrastructure – so it's worth checking to be sure. Wi-Fi network can be protected from breaches by hackers by changing the name of the wireless access point or router, also known as the Service Set Identifier (SSID). Also it should be use a complex Pre-shared Key (PSK) passphrase for additional security.

- Ensure a strong password policy: must be ensured that all employees use a strong password on all devices that contain sensitive information. A strong password is at least 15 characters in length – ideally more – and contains a mix of upper- and lower-case letters, numbers, and symbols. The more difficult it is to crack a password, the less likely a brute force attack will be successful. Should also put in place a policy to change passwords at regular intervals, at least quarterly. As an additional measure, small businesses should enable multi-factor authentication (MFA) on employees' devices and apps.

- Use password managers: Using strong passwords which are unique to every device or account quickly becomes difficult to remember. The need to remember and type out lengthy passwords each time can also slow employees down. That's why many businesses use password management tools. A password manager stores passwords for employees, automatically generating the correct username, password and even security question answers that need to log into websites or apps. This means users only have to remember a single PIN or master password to access their vault of login information. Many password managers also guide users away from weak or re-used passwords and remind to change them regularly.

- Use a firewall: A firewall protects hardware as well as software, which is a benefit to any company with its own physical servers. A firewall also works by blocking or deterring viruses from entering the network. This is in contrast to an antivirus which works by targeting the software affected by a virus that has already gotten through. Ensuring a firewall is in place protects business's network traffic – both inbound and outbound. It can stop hackers from attacking your network by blocking certain websites. It can also be programmed so that sending out sensitive data and confidential emails from company's network is restricted. Once a firewall is installed, is important to remember to keep it up-to-date. By checking regularly that it has the latest updates for software or firmware.

- Use a Virtual Private Network (VPN): A Virtual Private Network provides another layer of security for business. VPNs allow employees to access company's network securely when working remotely or travelling. They do this by funnelling data and IP address through another secure connection in between own internet connection and the actual website or online service that needs to access. They are especially useful when using public internet connections – such as in coffee shops, airports, or Airbnb's – which can be vulnerable to hackers. A VPN gives users a secure connection which separates hackers from the data they are hoping to steal.

-    Guard against physical theft: While the company need to be mindful of hackers trying to breach your network, must not be forget that hardware can be stolen too. Unauthorized individuals should be prevented from gaining access to business devices such as laptops, PCs, scanners, and so on. This may include physically securing the device or adding a physical tracker to recover the device in case of loss or theft. Ensure all employees understand the importance of any data that might be stored on their cell phones or laptops when out and about. For devices used by multiple employees, is important to consider creating separate user accounts and profiles for additional protection. It's also a good idea to set up remote wiping – this allows to remotely delete the data on a lost or stolen device.

-    Don't overlook mobile devices: Mobile devices create security challenges, especially if they hold sensitive information or can access the corporate network. Yet they can sometimes be overlooked when businesses are planning their cybersecurity. It is important to ask employees to password-protect their mobile devices, install security apps, and encrypt their data to stop criminals from stealing information while the phone is on public networks. It is essentials to be sure to set reporting procedures for lost or stolen phones and tablets.

-    Ensure third parties who deal with the business are also secure: the owner must be wary of other businesses such as partners or suppliers who may be granted access to your systems. It is important to make sure they are following similar practices to you. the business should be afraid to check before it grants access to anybody.

For many small businesses, cybersecurity is not necessarily their core focus. It's understandable if small business need help with cybersecurity. Here are some key attributes to look out for:

- Independent tests and reviews: A cybersecurity company could dazzle small business with technical jargon and an impressive marketing campaign, so it's important to look at independent tests and reviews. The best cybersecurity firms want their products tested and are happy to share the results.

- Avoid cheap options: Small business owners want to avoid a company that comes in, installs software and then disappears. Additionally, a company claiming to specialize only in one field without offering additional products or support can't provide the protection small business need.

- Extra support: Whether a threat has been detected or small business is having trouble backing up files, a small business wants a company that offers a decent level of support. Is important to choose a company that helps small business to navigate threats, finds solutions, and takes the hassle out of cybersecurity.

- Growth potential: As the business grows, small business needs a cybersecurity company that can grow with you. it is important to focus on companies that offer a full range of security systems for businesses, including those small business may need in the future.

Small business owners have always had long to-do lists, but now, cybersecurity is at the top of the list. Fortunately, there are steps small business can take to protect against those threats, and the right cybersecurity company can help mitigate those risks, if the business itself is not in the range of possibility to act internally, very difficult for a small/medium size business.

Given the increased cyber security risk for businesses, the significance of security is rising. Fundamentally, as modern society has become more technologically dependent than ever, with no signs of slowing down, data leaks that could end in identity theft are now publicly published on different social media accounts. In addition, sensitive details like credit card information, social security numbers, and bank account details are now held in cloud storage services like Google Drive and Dropbox, making it easier for cybercriminals to misuse them. And it is the harsh reality that no matter whether a small business, individual or multinational giant, everyone counts on computer networks daily. It further gets aggravated by the advancement in cloud services, inadequate cloud service protection, smartphones, the Internet of Things (IoT), and multiple possible security susceptibilities that didn't exist a few years ago. Thus, governments worldwide focus more on cybercrimes and making organizations aware of cybersecurity best practices for small businesses.

# 1.3 CYBER SECURITY IN THE LARGE BUSINESS

In this modern, technologically advanced world, cyber security has become necessary for companies of all sizes as their networks and computer systems possessing confidential and worthwhile data have become exposed to malicious actors. Without a comprehensive cyber security strategy, an organization cannot guard itself against cyber security threats leaving it vulnerable to cyber criminals, who will pinpoint those companies as easy targets. And as technology has evolved tremendously over the years, so have the cyber threats and the need for cybersecurity for business. Cyber security for businesses is a preventive measure designed to safeguard online data from theft and damage. Given this comprehensive safety feature, almost every modern business adopted cybersecurity, and the need for professionals who have completed formal online IT Security training courses has increased dramatically. Main focus for large business is to tackle cyber-security by having strong and strict polices in place and by informing and training employees on security issues. In simple words, cyber security refers to a series of procedures and techniques to guard a business's essential systems and confidential data against cyber threats and online data infringements, i.e., cybercrime. In addition, cyber-attacks are increasingly becoming more advanced as criminals are having an easier time penetrating through conventional security controls by executing new techniques of attack that execute social engineering and AI. As they adopt the latest technology, companies must also improve their cyber security efforts and look for the best cyber security software for businesses that can guard them against all these potential cyber threats. By a "CIO insight" statistic published in 2017, 94% of large American business have a cyber-security policy in place. Across the world several large companies have recently suffered from cyber-attacks, resulting in a breach of security and leaking of sensitive information to the public. As the public is more aware of the situation the biggest loss for the enterprise is the loss of customer trust as it happened already in the past with big loss of customer after those events with a consequential loss of money. In 2018 the European union decide to strengthening with a new General Data Protection Regulation, that will be discussed in the following chapter, as before that companies could hide behind closed doors when recovering from a breach, now the company could be fine up to 4% of their annual turnover, in consequence the company will take more actions to prevent those breaches. For large enterprise the major security threat are the employees. That compared with small and medium business this risk is much greater. As it was describe in the previous paragraph there are several way that an enterprise could be under attack. To put in place all the measures on the threats that we describe before we need to have several pillar in large enterprise. Such as effective training and have in place a mature security culture[8].

- Effective training. As described in the previous paragraph there are many threats that large business are facing in an evolving cyber world. The majority of the threats are affecting the human factor in the enterprise and in large business this risk is multiply buy the number of employees, more employees more possibility to be caught in one of those traps. Software are made to be perfect and with update the developer try to make it more effective, humans on the other end are far from perfection. Humans are the weakest link in cyber security so the duty of the employer is to train the employees and minimize the possibility falling in the hackers traps.

- Mature security culture. Security culture is the collection of the beliefs, perceptions and values that employees share in relation to risks within an organization. A security culture must be in place to standardize the operation, to improve based on experience and to work together in non-regular basis without reducing security standards. Let`s see now this three in details. By standardizing the operation of the employees is fundamental because in this way is minimize the possibility of self-thought actions to lead to threats, of course is not always possible because this will make the job too automatic. Improving based on experience is one of the most important thing to do in cyber security, is a new world always changing and improving, hackers are finding every day way to access our information and only buy doing mistake and report those mistakes the employer will find a way to minimize the possibility to ending up again in those traps. Something very important too is to work together in non-regular basis without reducing security standard, this is essential as the employee will find him/her self in non-normal situation multiple times during his/her history as worker, essential is to never reduce security standards to avoid for example repetitive actions, as the employee might think it is not necessary, or to skip steps in our everyday procedure, this will drastically reduce the security standards. A mantra to remember in those cases is that if those procedure are in place in that particular way there is a reason behind, usually they are the result of a security risk assessment, if the employee should find any procedure not necessary or out of date, he/she should report this straight away to a superior and the superior should analyse the report of the employee and try to understand if it is possible to do something about or if is the best procedure to avoid the threats, would be nice in this case from the responsible a feedback to the employee who report the problem, time permitting. If instead there is a poor security culture the employees will have an active resistance to the security program, retaliation from managers or other employees against person who reported Safety issue and low number of hazard reports. A resistance from the employees to the security programme will lead the employees to refuse those procedures putted in place to protect as much as possible the enterprise from attacks and instead will lead to employees self-actions with consequential loss of data, money and costumer trust. This resistance to the security program will lead the employees that actually follow the security program in difficult position towards the colleagues who don`t follow the program with consequential retaliation or/and isolation. This will lead to low number of security report, even though could be interpreted as good sign a low number of security is actually the opposite, because this is a sign of not reporting what should be reported, it could be mistaken with absence of threats. In today's world is impossible to have a low number of threats for many reasons, more in particular for the big enterprise where there is an high number of employees and high number of digitalization within the structure. This always make the enterprise an easy target. As we said couple of times already the only way to minimize the damage in this fast changing world is to report every single accident, incident or even the sensation that something was not right, this is the only way to have an effective procedure in place to minimize the possibility of future cyber-attacks. So to have a mature security culture the employer must have in place a strong hazard reporting culture, lack of repeat security incidents, low number of high risk issues and security issues and corrective actions are completed on time.

Big enterprise had to do something to contain the possibility to be attacked by an hacker, this is the reason why new professional figures are born, such us the cyber security manager and the chief information security officer (CISO). Those new role are completely new and very difficult to find as we talk about a very new environment constantly evolving. We will now describe them[9]:

-       Cyber security manager is a professional role that can deeply help an enterprise to defend the cyber structure. The market of cyber security is in constant grow as there are more and more enterprise who want to defend them self by investing in effective and complete protection systems. The Cyber Security Manager is responsible for managing the security of a company's IT systems, outlining a defence plan, monitoring infrastructure and processes and coordinating the teams in charge. Evaluate what are the useful precautions to adopt and know all the risks and threats that the activity may face. It is a professional figure who has begun to establish itself in parallel with the growth of Digital Transformation and now plays a key role in a world where the circulation of data and information is preponderant and crucial. The chances of becoming the target of an attack are very high and relying on an IT security expert is a real lifesaver for all companies that want to work in peace while guaranteeing Business Continuity. Specifically, it monitors the integrity of all the tools implemented, carries out supervision activities and collaborates in the creation of policies and guidelines for all personnel. It is the point of reference, within a business, for everything concerning safety and has a technical but also managerial and consultancy role. Some of the duties and responsibility are: he/she prepares the measures and behaviours useful for preventing cyber-attacks. He/she will analyse the enterprise computer systems to identify flaws and vulnerabilities. Will check the effectiveness of defence tools and antiviruses. Verify that everything is working properly and that what is in charge is appropriate for the business. Protect the privacy of data and information by developing a strategy that maximizes its integrity, availability and confidentiality. It intervenes in the event of cyber-attacks, accidents, failures or errors. Outlines recovery and emergency response plans. Adjust the entire business to legal standards related to security, managing regulatory compliance and defining policies. And finally be responsible for staff training and ensures that everyone observes established standards and behaviours.

In Italy to occupy this role the candidate should have a bachelor computer science or informatic engineering and then specialize in Cyber Security by integrating training with specific in-depth courses.

In this way it is possible to acquire all the technical knowledge necessary to carry out the role with seriousness and professionalism. In particular, a Cyber Security Manager must know how to plan, implement and review IT security projects, using their knowledge of programming and software testing. Must know all techniques and tools related to Vulnerability Management and know how to implement and manage Identity and Access Management systems. Be familiar with leading attack simulation tools and familiar with common tools and frameworks. He/she must also be able to manage the budget and have perfect knowledge of regulations and standards related to safety (ISO/IEC). Among the soft skills it is useful to have good management, relationship and communication skills, to be punctual and precise and to have a good predisposition for updating and training.

-       The CISO (chief information security officer) has the task of defining the correct strategies to best protect corporate assets and mitigate IT risks: it is therefore an important figure in the corporate organization chart.

Among the most requested professions in 2018, by all now considered as the year of information security, there is certainly that of the CISO, Chief Information Security Officer, that is, an information security manager capable of defining the right strategy of protection of corporate assets and mitigate all possible IT risks. Taking into account the continuous evolution of IT threats, the CISO therefore represents a fundamental figure for corporate IT security, especially in light of the new European regulations for the protection of data, networks and information systems: the GDRP and the NIS directive. The presence of an information security manager correctly inserted in the company organization chart should, if not eliminate, at least limit the occurrence of a data breach. Despite everything, however, a study carried out by the Information Security & Privacy Observatory of the Milan Polytechnic at the end of 2017 showed that the figure of the CISO is formalized only in 46% of Italian companies, while in 12% of cases it is actually present even if it is not officially contemplated. Most of the time, then, the CISO reports to the CIO (Chief Information Officer) and more rarely interfaces directly with the owners and with the Board of Directors. In addition to the obvious technical skills in information security acquired in the field, the CISO can also obtain a specific certification such as the one offered by the EC-Council. In particular, the C|CISO (Certified CISO) program is divided into five application fields providing the related technical and application skills summarized in:

1. Governance.

Define, implement, manage and maintain an information security governance program. Create an information security management structure. Create a framework for monitoring information security governance taking into account cost-benefit analyses of controls and ROI (Return on Investment). Understand the standards, procedures, directives, policies, regulations and legal issues affecting the information security program. Know the different standards such as the ISO 27000 series. Security Risk Management, Controls, Audit Management. Identify operational processes and business objectives to assess the level of risk tolerance. Design information system controls in line with operational needs and objectives and conduct testing prior to implementation to ensure effectiveness and efficiency. Identify and select the resources needed to effectively implement and maintain controls over information systems. Design and implement controls on information systems to mitigate risk. Design and conduct testing of information security controls to ensure effectiveness, identify deficiencies, and ensure alignment with organization policies, standards, and procedures. Understand the IT audit process and be familiar with IT audit standards. Apply information systems audit principles, skills and techniques to examine and test information systems technologies and applications in order to design and implement a thorough risk-based IT audit strategy. Perform the audit process according to established standards and interpret the results based on defined criteria to ensure that information systems are protected, controlled and effective in supporting the organization's objectives. Ensure that necessary changes based on audit findings are implemented effectively and in a timely manner

2. Security Risk Management, Controls, Audit Management.

Identify operational processes and business objectives to assess the level of risk tolerance. Design information system controls in line with operational needs and objectives and conduct testing prior to implementation to ensure effectiveness and efficiency. Identify and select the resources needed to effectively implement and maintain controls over information systems. Design and implement controls on information systems to mitigate risk. Design and conduct testing of information security controls to ensure effectiveness, identify deficiencies, and ensure alignment with organization policies, standards, and procedures. Understand the IT audit process and be familiar with IT audit standards. Apply information systems audit principles, skills and techniques to examine and test information systems technologies and applications in order to design and implement a thorough risk-based IT audit strategy. Perform the audit process according to established standards and interpret the results based on defined criteria to ensure that information systems are protected, controlled and effective in supporting the organization's objectives. Ensure that necessary changes based on audit findings are implemented effectively and in a timely manner.

3. Security Program Management & Operations

Define the activities required to successfully execute the information security project. Develop, manage and monitor the program budget of information systems, estimate and control the costs of individual projects

Identify, negotiate, acquire, and manage the resources necessary for successful information systems program design and implementation (e.g., people, infrastructure, and architecture). Acquire, develop and manage an information security project team. Direct information security personnel and establish communication and teamwork between the information systems team and other security personnel

4. Information Security Core Concepts.

Identify the criteria for mandatory and discretionary data access control, understand the different factors that help in implementing access controls, and design an access control plan. Identify different access control systems, such as ID cards and biometrics. Understand different social engineering concepts and their role in attacks targeting corporate employees to develop best practices to counter them. Develop an identity theft response plan. Identify and design a plan to overcome phishing attacks. Identify risk mitigation and treatment processes and understand the concept of acceptable risk. Identify the resources needed to implement the risk management plan. Design a systematic and structured risk assessment process and establish, in coordination with stakeholders, an IT security risk management program based on standards and procedures. Develop, coordinate and manage risk management teams. Understand the residual risk in the information infrastructure. Assess threats and vulnerabilities to identify security risks and regularly update applicable security controls. Develop, implement and monitor business continuity plans in the event of disruptive events and ensure alignment with organizational goals and purpose. Identify vulnerabilities and attacks associated with wireless networks and manage different security tools for wireless networks. Assess the threat of viruses, trojans and malware to the organization's security and identify sources and means of malware infection.

5. Strategic Planning, Finance & Vendor Management

Perform external analyses of the organization (for example, analyses of customers, competitors, markets and the industrial environment) and internal analyses (risk management, organizational capabilities, performance measurement) and use them to align the information security program with the objectives of the organization. Evaluate and adjust IT investments to ensure they are on track to support the organization's strategic objectives. Acquire and manage the resources necessary for the implementation and management of the information security plan. Monitor and oversee cost management of information security projects, return on investment (ROI) of major IT infrastructure and security related purchases, and ensure alignment with strategic plan.

In general, therefore, it is understood that it is appropriate for the CISO to hold a managerial and executive position within the company. His/her main task is to ensure that security initiatives are consistent with corporate programs and business objectives, ensuring that the information assets and technologies used are adequately protected.

So to conclude this paragraph on the cyber security in large business we have a main weakness when it comes to this type of business, people. In this particular case employees, this liability can`t be removed but instead it can be managed by following some procedures as describe above.

Below are examples of some prominent global companies impacted by cyber-attacks and data breaches[10].

- eBay, In March 2014, eBay, a leading eCommerce giant, was the victim of an infringement of encrypted passwords, costing more than 145 million eBay users to reset their passwords. In addition, cybercriminals used a small group of employee passwords to access user data. The misappropriated data included encrypted passwords and other confidential details, including email addresses, names, phone numbers, physical addresses, and dates of birth. The breach was proclaimed in May 2014 after a month-long probe by eBay.

- Yahoo announced that a cyberattack in 2013 by a group of cybercriminals had compromised over 1 billion user accounts. In this example, security answers and questions were also jeopardized, raising the threat of identity theft. Yahoo initially reported the infringement in 2016, and it caused all affected users to modify passwords and re-enter any unencrypted safety answers and questions to make them end-to-end encrypted in the future.

# 1.4 CYBER SECURITY IN SMALL AND MEDIUM BUSINESS

In small and medium business we have some main differences compared with the large business. This differences are present because of the different characteristic of the two types of enterprises. Starting with the different size of the business, this bring many factors to change and behave in a different way. Such as the amount of employees, as it was described in the previous paragraph more employee we have more possibility of having a vulnerability, in terms of possible mistake that the employee could giving access to someone not authorised. With the increasing of number of employee it increase also the difficulties of doing an effective training to all of them against the risk of cyber-attacks and in general with smaller amount of employees it will be easier to have a strong security culture in place. Smaller enterprise are not only beneficial for the amount of employees but also is reduce to the minimum the possibility of being target of cyber-attacks with a political goals, as will have a smaller media impact, so the desire of an hacker to make an attack with political goal will be almost unnecessary. In smaller enterprise also the number of device used will be drastically lower, reducing in this way the weakness from where the hacker could access the files. Not only devices and employees number will be reduced compared to a big enterprise but also the number of all others stakeholders will be lower, such as customers or less connected enterprise that will work together to achieve the final objective, to summarize less customers less data to collect so less vulnerability to be attacked. Small and medium business will also have lower number of law and rules to follow, GDPR apply in full also for small business. To comply with these principles, the first step in lawfully gathering this data is to receive consent from data subjects, which is a cornerstone of the GDPR. Even if is a sole trader, a small business with 10-20 employees, or a medium-sized business with 200-250 employees, the GDPR must be followed. If the business have less than 250 employees, GDPR requires to keep internal records of processing activities, because the data being processed could jeopardise someone's rights and freedoms, where the data relates to criminal convictions and the special categories of data, and where the organisation processes data on a regular basis. On the other side all of this will lower the level of alertness of those types of business, as they will think it is not necessary to protect against a threat that they don't see. Very important in this case is to train and raise sensibility between managers and owners of this type of business to take all precaution possible to protect their activities. As there is no legal requirement yet for them to put in place all possible precautions, very important is the role of the government to make available all possible information and training to this small and medium business, many countries are following this recommendations by making free access web site were to have basic training. Like in United kingdom where is possible to access the government website to have more and detailed information. But what should actually change is the mentality and culture of all business owner in putting the cyber security as top priority investment, never should be forgotten that even a small gym or doctor office are in possession of everyone data and as it was described in the chapter before all type of data is a vulnerability that could be attack. In the following chapter it will be describe GDPR in details. So as it was said already small business are just as at risk from cyber security threats as large enterprises. A common misconception for small businesses is an idea of security through obscurity, that your business is too small to be a target, but unfortunately, this is not the case. Attacks are evolving day by day and one of the new threats are the automate attacks, this type of attacks are increasing drastically in number, it's easy for the attackers with this type of automate attacks to target hundreds, if not thousands of small businesses at once. For the reason describe above small businesses often have less stringent technological defences, less awareness of threats and less time and resource to put into cybersecurity. This makes them an easier target for hackers than bigger organizations. But, at the same time, they are no less lucrative targets. Even the very smallest businesses can deal with large sums of money, or have access to huge amounts of customer data, which, under regulations such as GDPR, they are obligated to protect. Small businesses also often work with larger companies, and so they can be used by hackers as a way to target those companies. In realty small business have the most to lose from being attacks as when in the last years where analysed the amount of money lost after a cyber-attack the number was always in millions of euros, no thousand, and a smaller business will have less capacity to rebound a big loss like that. This is why small business must be aware of the threats and how to stop them. In the previous paragraph it was describe some types of cyber-attacks and how to fight them now we are going to focus on the most common in a small business[11].

- Phishing attack: The biggest, most damaging and most widespread threat facing small businesses is phishing attacks. Phishing accounts for 90% of all breaches that organizations face, they've grown 65% over the last year, and they account for over 12 billion euros in business losses. Phishing attacks occur when an attacker pretends to be a trusted contact, and entices a user to click a malicious link, download a malicious file, or give them access to sensitive information, account details or credentials. In recent years there was a much more sophisticated grown, with attackers becoming more convincing in pretending to be legitimate business contacts. There has also been a rise in Business Email Compromise, which involves bad actors using phishing campaigns to steal business email account passwords from high level executives, and then using these accounts to fraudulently request payments from employees. As we describe in the previous paragraph the weakest link in cyber security is the human being and this type of attack concentre all social engineering in finding way to target humans within business, rather than technological weaknesses. However, there are technological defences against phishing attacks. There are some software that can minimise the phishing email to reach the employees inboxes. Those solutions allow users to report phishing emails and then allow admins to delete them from all users inboxes. Another very important way to prevent phishing email is the multi factor authenticator also known as MFA. MFA applies an extra layer of security to the authentication process when users log into an account. This is commonly delivered as a SMS-code, tap notification on a trusted device, or biometric check, such as a fingerprint or FaceID scan. With this type of security even if an attacker is able to compromise an account username and password using phishing methods, they would still be unable to access your account without that additional piece of information, known only to the user. The final barrier to protect emails from phishing is the security awareness training as it was describe already in the previous paragraph.

-        Malware Attacks: Malware is the second big threat facing small businesses. It encompasses a variety of cyber threats such as trojans and viruses. Malware is a varied term for malicious code that hackers create to gain access to networks, steal data, or destroy data on computers. Malware usually comes from malicious website downloads, spam emails or from connecting to other infected machines or devices. These attacks are particularly damaging for small businesses because they can cripple devices, which requires expensive repairs or replacements to fix. They can also give attackers a back door to access data, which can put customers and employees at risk. Small businesses are more likely to employ people who use their own devices for work, as it helps to save time and cost. This, however, increases their likelihood of suffering from a malware attack, as personal devices are much more likely to be at risk from malicious downloads. Business can prevent malware attacks by having strong technological defences in place. Endpoint Protection solutions protect devices from malware downloads and give admins a central control panel to manage devices and ensure all users' security is up to date. Web Security is also important, stopping users from visiting malicious webpages and downloading malicious software.

- Ransomware: Ransomware is one of the most common cyber-attacks, hitting thousands of businesses every year. These attacks have only become more common, as they are one of the most lucrative forms of attacks. Ransomware involves encrypting company data so that it cannot be used or accessed, and then forcing the company to pay a ransom to unlock the data. This leaves businesses with a tough choice to pay the ransom and potentially lose huge sums of money, or cripple their services with a loss of data. Small businesses are especially at risk from these types of attack. Reports have shown 71% of ransomware attacks target small businesses, with an average ransom demand of $116,000. Attackers know that smaller businesses are much more likely to pay a ransom, as their data is often not backed-up and they need to be up and running as soon as possible. The healthcare sector is particularly badly hit by this type of attack, as locking patient medical records and appointment times can damage a business to a point where it has no choice but to close, unless a ransom has been paid. To prevent these attacks, businesses need to have strong Endpoint Protection in place across all business devices. These will help to stop ransomware attacks from being able to effectively encrypt data. Endpoint protection solution SentinelOne even provides a 'ransomware rollback' feature, which allows organizations to very quickly detect and mitigate against ransomware attacks. Businesses should also consider having an effective cloud back-up solution in place. These solutions back up company data securely in the cloud, helping to mitigate against data loss. There are various methods of data back-up available to organizations, so it's important to research the method that will work best for your organization. The benefit of implementing data back-up and recovery is that in the event of a ransomware attack, IT teams can quickly recover their data without having to pay any ransoms, or lose productivity. This is an important step towards improved cyber resilience.

- Weak passwords: Another big threat facing small businesses is employees using weak or easily guessed passwords. Many small businesses use multiple cloud based services, that require different accounts. These services often can contain sensitive data and financial information. Using easily guessed passwords, or using the same passwords for multiple accounts, can cause this data to become compromised. Small businesses are often at risk from compromises that come from employees using weak passwords, due to an overall lack of awareness about the damage they can cause. An average of 19% of enterprise professionals use easily guessed passwords or share passwords across accounts. To ensure that employees are using strong passwords, users should consider Business Password Management technologies. These platforms help employees to manage passwords for all their accounts, suggesting strong passwords that cannot be easily cracked. Businesses should also consider implementing

Multi-Factor Authentication technologies. As previously mentioned, these solutions ensure that users need more than just a password to have access to business accounts. This includes enforcing multiple verification steps, such as a passcode sent to a mobile device. These security controls help to prevent attackers from accessing business accounts, even if they do correctly crack a weak password.

- Insider threats: The final major threat facing small businesses is the insider threat. An insider threat is a risk to an organization that is caused by the actions of employees, former employees, business contractors or associates. These actors can access critical data about your company, and they can case harmful effects through greed or malice, or simply through ignorance and carelessness. Verizon found that 25% of data breaches were caused by insider threats. This is a growing problem and can put employees and customers at risk, or cause the company financial damage. Within small businesses, insider threats are growing as more employees have access to multiple accounts, that hold more data. Research has found that 62% of employees have reported having access to accounts that they probably didn't need to. To block insider threats, small businesses need to ensure that they have a strong culture of security awareness within their organization. This will help to stop insider threats caused by ignorance, and help employees to spot early on when an attacker has compromised, or is attempting to compromise company data.

Small business at the moment are facing a range of threats. There are different way to protect this business but the best way is to have a comprehensive set of security tools and rules in place, also utilize security awareness training to ensure that users are aware of security threats and hot to prevent them. If a business owner or a manager is not able to put in place a security system to prevent this attacks alone he/she should get advice from an expert in cyber security. Right now is not something obliged by the law so is really about the sensibility of the manager/owner but for sure this is the best investment that in a new era of cyber threats small and medium business could make.

Everything in the world has moved online in the digital age that we currently live in. We use the internet to help us do tasks for data storage or information access. We are more vulnerable to online attacks as our involvement in the digital world grows. Digital security tips can be helpful in such situations. There is no question that the rate of growth of cybercrime is exponential. The criminals or "hackers" of the World Wide Web are accessing and using the personal data of internet users.

- Easily Accessible System: Protecting a system from data breaches that require sophisticated technologies is frequently difficult or impossible. Security can only be jeopardized when hackers have easy access to the system. Hackers with advanced skills can gain unauthorized access by defeating speech recognition, retinal scans, and access codes. They can breach the system's firewall and trick the biometric system.

- Lack of Diverse Systems: One of the main causes of cyberattacks is that computers are known to hold vast amounts of data in a limited amount of space. Cybercrime was developed following the invention of computers. A little storage area makes it simpler for hackers to grab and use data for their gain quickly. Therefore, it is advisable to separate the data and not keep it all on the system at once.

- Coding Errors: Operating systems, which are constructed with millions of lines of code, are what allow computers to run. Operating systems are created by human developers, leaving the software susceptible to mistakes. The smallest loophole in the coding might not significantly impact how the operating system works, but cybercriminals can quickly exploit these holes.

- Lack of Maintenance: Anything we overlook and dismiss as simple might become a serious problem. The same principles apply to cybercrime. Small business might get into a lot of trouble if they don't take care to keep their system secure. A little carelessness on their part could open the door to cybercriminals.

Cybersecurity is essential because it protects all forms of data from loss and theft. Intellectual property, personally identifiable information (PII), sensitive data, protected health information (PHI), individually identifiable information (PII), sensitive data, and corporate and government information systems are all included. If cyber security professionals did not continuously endeavour to thwart denial-of-service attacks, it would be almost impossible to use many websites. It is essential and in everyone's best interest to have sophisticated cyber defence plans and methods to protect this data. Everyone depends on essential infrastructures, such as power plants, hospitals, and other healthcare facilities. To keep our society functioning, we require these. Cybersecurity breaches can result in identity theft and extortion attempts on an individual level, which can seriously harm that person's life. Cyber security recommendations are vital to helping you develop a better understanding of cyber security.

# 1.5 CYBERATTACK DEFINITION

A cyberattack is a malicious and deliberate attempt by an individual or organization to breach the information system of another individual or organization[12]. Usually, the attacker seeks some type of benefit from disrupting the victim's network. Cyberattacks hit businesses every day. Former Cisco CEO John Chambers once said, "There are two types of companies: those that have been hacked, and those who don't yet know they have been hacked." According to the Cisco Annual Cybersecurity Report, the total volume of events has increased almost fourfold between January 2016 and October 2017. Cybercrime has increased every year as people try to benefit from vulnerable business systems. Often, attackers are looking for ransom: 53 percent of cyberattacks resulted in damages of 500,000 euros or more. Cyberthreats can also be launched with ulterior motives. Some attackers look to obliterate systems and data as a form of "hacktivism." A botnet is a network of devices that has been infected with malicious software, such as a virus. Attackers can control a botnet as a group without the owner's knowledge with the goal of increasing the magnitude of their attacks. Often, a botnet is used to overwhelm systems in a distributed-denial-of-service attack (DDoS) attack.

Malware is a term used to describe malicious software, including spyware, ransomware, viruses, and worms. Malware breaches a network through a vulnerability, typically when a user clicks a dangerous link or email attachment that then installs risky software. Once inside the system, malware can do the following:

- Blocks access to key components of the network (ransomware)
- Installs malware or additional harmful software
- Covertly obtains information by transmitting data from the hard drive (spyware)
- Disrupts certain components and renders the system inoperable

Phishing is the practice of sending fraudulent communications that appear to come from a reputable source, usually through email. The goal is to steal sensitive data like credit card and login information or to install malware on the victim's machine. Phishing is an increasingly common cyberthreat.

Man-in-the-middle (MitM) attacks, also known as eavesdropping attacks, occur when attackers insert themselves into a two-party transaction. Once the attackers interrupt the traffic, they can filter and steal data. Two common points of entry for MitM attacks:

- On unsecure public Wi-Fi, attackers can insert themselves between a visitor's device and the network. Without knowing, the visitor passes all information through the attacker.
- Once malware has breached a device, an attacker can install software to process all of the victim's information.

A denial-of-service attack floods systems, servers, or networks with traffic to exhaust resources and bandwidth. As a result, the system is unable to fulfill legitimate requests. Attackers can also use multiple compromised devices to launch this attack. This is known as a distributed-denial-of-service (DDoS) attack.

A Structured Query Language (SQL) injection occurs when an attacker inserts malicious code into a server that uses SQL and forces the server to reveal information it normally would not. An attacker could carry out a SQL injection simply by submitting malicious code into a vulnerable website search box. Learn how to defend against SQL injection attacks.

A zero-day exploit hits after a network vulnerability is announced but before a patch or solution is implemented. Attackers target the disclosed vulnerability during this window of time. Zero-day vulnerability threat detection requires constant awareness.

Some example of the most famous cyberattacks:

- Check Point Research (CPR) has released information on cyberattacks that have been seen in the context of the ongoing Russia-Ukraine conflict. In the first three days of battle, cyberattacks on Ukraine's government and military sector increased by an astounding 196%. The number of cyberattacks on Russian businesses has climbed by 4%. Phishing emails in East Slavic languages grew sevenfold, with a third of those malicious phishing emails being sent from Ukrainian email addresses to Russian receivers.

- A severe remote code execution (RCE) vulnerability in the Apache logging package Log4j 2 versions 2.14.1 and below was reported on December 9th 2021 (CVE-2021-44228). With over 400,000 downloads from its GitHub repository, Apache Log4j is the most popular java logging package. It is used by a large number of enterprises throughout the world and allows users to log in to a variety of popular applications. It's easy to exploit this flaw, which allows threat actors to take control of java-based web servers and perform remote code execution assaults.

- The world is now facing what seems to be a 5th generation cyber-attack, a sophisticated, multi-vector attack with clear characteristics of the cyber pandemic. Named Sunburst by researchers, we believe this is one of the most sophisticated and severe attacks ever seen. The attack has been reported to impact major US government offices as well as many private sector organizations.

This series of attacks was made possible when hackers were able to embed a backdoor into SolarWinds software updates. Over 18,000 companies and government offices downloaded what seemed to be a regular software update on their computers, but was actually a Trojan horse. By leveraging a common IT practice of software updates, the attackers utilized the backdoor to compromise the organization's assets enabling them to spy on the organization and access its data. Cyber threats are now a reality for businesses. Cybercriminals are aware of recent advancements in company cybersecurity and have adapted their attacks to circumvent and defeat traditional safeguards. To avoid detection, modern cyberattacks are multi-vectored and use polymorphic code. As a result, detecting and responding to threats is more challenging than ever. Cybercriminals' primary target and an organization's first line of defence in the remote work world is the endpoint. Securing the remote workforce necessitates an understanding of the most common cyber risks that employees experience, as well as endpoint security solutions capable of detecting, preventing, and resolving these assaults. Cyberattacks come in a variety of different forms. Cybercriminals use many different methods to launch a cyberattack, a phishing attack, an exploitation of compromised credentials, and more. From this initial access, cybercriminals can go on to achieve different objectives including malware infections, ransomware, denial of service attack, data theft, and more.

The lasts trend of cyberattacks are in various range but here we have list of the main one[13]:

- In February 2022, Russia launched an invasion of Ukraine. This conflict used a variety of tactics, including attacks via land, sea, air, and cyberspace. Russia has a history of engaging in cyberattacks against Ukraine, including DDoS attacks and attacks against the country's power infrastructure in 2015 and 2022. With the invasion, cyberattacks, both official and unofficial, grew more common. On both sides of the conflict, volunteer troops launched various attacks against both military and civilian targets. Additionally, Russian APTs launched coordinated attacks to disrupt critical services within Ukraine. On the Ukrainian side, government representatives have officially requested and endorsed help with protecting the country's critical infrastructure and launching attacks against Russian targets. While state-sponsored APTs have historically launched politically motivated attacks, this conflict led to the engagement of cybercriminals and individuals in cyberattacks as well.

- Ransomware attacks have consistently grown to take on larger targets. Ransomware attacks began targeting individuals and moved to focus on large enterprises and organizations that can pay large ransoms. Recently, cyber threat actors have begun targeting entire countries with their attacks. As these ransomware groups grow larger and more visible, they are increasingly linked to nation-states. Large-scale organizations launching attacks against countries are difficult to hide from governments, so cybercrime groups like Conti are increasingly aligning themselves politically with nation-states to continue operating. As the United States and other jurisdictions move to crack down on law enforcement, some countries selectively cooperate, protecting cybercrime groups whose activities coincide with political interests.

- Supply chain attacks have become a top-of-mind security threat in recent years. Attacks such as those on SolarWinds and Kaseya brought them to prominence, and open-source software supply chain attacks pose a significant risk to organizations today. However, near-universal adoption of cloud infrastructure and the challenges that companies face securing their cloud environments make cloud supply chain attacks a significant risk in the near future. Attacks against third-party providers enable an attacker to dramatically scale and increase the effects of their attacks, as demonstrated by the alleged March 2022 attack on Okta. Similar attacks against a cloud provider, such as AWS or Azure, would have a much more significant impact.

-       As companies become more reliant on mobile communication, cyberattacks increasingly target mobile devices. While the NSO Group's Pegasus is the most famous threat to mobile devices, it is far from the only mobile malware. New mobile surveillance malware created by Cytrox and QuaDream have begun using the same techniques and providing the same capabilities as Pegasus. These three spyware variants have also begun using new vulnerabilities and exploits to evade new protections on iPhones. In addition to spyware, sophisticated mobile malware such as Flubot and Malibot have begun building mobile device botnets using smishing and similar techniques. Cyber threat actors are also targeting official app stores with malware that masquerades as an antivirus, productivity tool, or other desirable application and delivers info stealers, banking trojans, and other mobile malware.

A cyberattack is preventable. The key to cyber defence is an end-to-end cyber security architecture that is multi-layered and spans all networks, endpoint and mobile devices, and cloud. With the right architecture, business can consolidate management of multiple security layers, control policy through a single pane of glass. This lets you correlate events across all network environments, cloud services, and mobile infrastructures. In addition to architecture these key measures will prevent cyberattacks:

- Maintain security hygiene
- Choose prevention over detection
- Cover all attack vectors
- Implement the most advanced technologies
- Keep threat intelligence up to date

Not only is responsibility of the business owner but is also responsibility of the government to protect and inform as much as possible the business against those threats with efficient organizations and legislations.

# 2.1 USA CYBERSECURITY ORGANIZATION

All organizations, regardless of size, need to adopt a heightened posture when it comes to cybersecurity and protecting their most critical assets. Sophisticated cyber actors and nation-states exploit vulnerabilities to steal information and money and are developing capabilities to disrupt, destroy, or threaten the delivery of essential services. Implementing organizational cybersecurity best practices requires coordination across the organization from leadership to IT to communications and human resources. From governance to updating technology, cybersecurity requires a holistic approach that often starts with leadership directive. Protecting the cyber space is an essential aspect of business operations and must be integrated at all levels. In the use the main agency that deal with this is the CISA (Cybersecurity and infrastructure security agency)[14]. CISA offers tools, services, resources, and current information for businesses and organizations to implement key cybersecurity practices. CISA provides services across all of CISA's mission areas that are available to Federal Government; State, Local, Tribal and Territorial Government; Private Industry; Academia; NGO and Non-Profit; and General Public stakeholders. In light of the risk and potential consequences of cyber events, CISA strengthens the security and resilience of cyberspace, an important homeland security mission. Despite the perception of the United States (US) as a technological and innovation powerhouse, it lags behind many other modern industrialised nations in terms of internet access and connectivity. The International Telecommunication Union[15] ranked the US 28th in terms of the percentage of individuals using the internet in 2013, with 84% connected; US polling organisations yield similar values. While the vast majority of Americans have access to the internet, such connections are not necessarily of high quality. The US has committed itself to fostering technological innovation with strategic focus on increasing internet and broadband internet access. Worldwide, the US has been in the vanguard of developing cyber security policy and strategy. As early as 2003 its government issued the first national cyber security strategy; the first EU countries to publish similar documents that addressed aspects of cyber security were Germany in 2005 and Sweden in 2006. The National Strategy to Secure Cyberspace of 2003 established three strategic objectives for national cyberspace security: preventing cyberattacks against national critical infrastructures; reducing national vulnerability to cyberattacks; and minimising damage and recovery time from cyberattacks that do occur. Five national priorities were identified for attaining these goals: securing federal computer systems and networks; developing a response system; establishing a threat and vulnerability reduction programme; initiating an awareness and training programme for cyber security; and developing a system of international cooperation. Cyber security policy in the US to date has consisted of piecemeal measures; likewise, legislation is less comprehensive and more topically-focused. Over 50 statutes address various aspects of cyber security. Since no overarching framework legislation or national cyber security strategy is in place that synthesises these documents or comprehensively describes the current strategy, forming a clear understanding of overall strategic objectives and priorities for enhancing cyber security is a complicated task. Most of the existing documents address national priorities from narrower cyber security areas, which furthermore leads to variance in terms of priorities and structure, and also fails to specify how they link to or supersede other policy documents. For the most part, these documents do not describe how they fit into the overall national cyber security strategy. Broader national security and defence strategies also outline cyber security objectives. The 2010 National Security Strategy was the first US national security strategy to devote substantial attention to cyber threats; it also represented a change in the characterisation of cyber threats by the federal government, with emphasis shifting from non-state terrorism to state-sponsored activities and from a predominantly political to an economic concern. The current National Security Strategy acknowledges the growing danger of disruptive and even destructive cyberattacks, and communicates the US's intent to fortify the cyber security of critical infrastructure, increase investment in cyber capabilities, and 'impose costs' on malicious cyber actors. The document focuses particularly on the US's goal to promote international norms in cyberspace. The priorities set out by the National Security Strategy are supported in the National Intelligence Strategy of the United States of America (2014), which lists as one of the four mission objectives for the intelligence community the detection and understanding cyber threats to inform and enable national security decision making, cybersecurity, and cyber effects operations. The strategy reaffirms goals such as increasing partnerships and information-sharing, as well as advancing technological capabilities. The US federal government's bureaucracy is vast and complicated; the exact number of agencies, offices, boards, and commissions is unknown. All federal departments and agencies are in charge of the protection of their own ICT systems, and many have sector-specific responsibilities for critical infrastructure for which they are responsible. The regulatory mandate of different departments and agencies varies; most departments have a generalised responsibility to regulate in their constituency, others have existing cyber security-specific regulations, while some do not have a clear authority to regulate cyber security. In such cases, some comply with high-level requirements, while others follow voluntary guidance. Moreover, in some cases, cyber security strategy documents assign high-level roles and responsibilities to federal government entities, but leave the implementation details to the agencies' discretion. As an example, criticism has been voiced that OMB and DHS roles and responsibilities for overseeing agencies' information security programmes have not been clearly or adequately defined. In respect to domestic crisis management, DHS provides crisis management and technical assistance to other federal government entities and the private sector. While crisis response coordination is centralised in the federal government, the execution is decentralised with each of the cyber incident response partners playing a legally mandated role. Public and private sector organisations are responsible for the preparedness activities and maintaining response capabilities and recovery actions. These capabilities, actions, roles and responsibilities are described in the DHS's strategic framework[16] for operational coordination and execution, the National Cyber Incident Response Plan. In addition to the DHS, key roles are played by the White House, DoD, NSA, DoJ, Federal Bureau of Investigation (FBI), DoS, sector-specific agencies (SSAs), other federal and state, local, tribal and territorial governments, as well as the private and non-governmental sectors, and international partners. DHS also houses an Office for Infrastructure Protection which leads the efforts to secure critical infrastructure, particularly focusing on government cooperating with the private sector infrastructure operators.

Responding to corporate failures and fraud that resulted in substantial financial losses to institutional and individual investors, Congress passed the Sarbanes Oxley Act in 2002[17]. The Act contains provisions affecting corporate governance, risk management, auditing, and financial reporting of public companies, including provisions intended to deter and punish corporate accounting fraud and corruption. For what regards data protection there is not a single principal data protection legislation in the united states. Rather, a jumble of hundreds of laws enacted both the federal and the state levels serve to protect the personal data of U.S. residents. At the federal level, the Federal Trade commission act broadly empowers the U.S. Federal trade commission (FTC) to bring enforcement actions to protect consumers against unfair or deceptive practices and to enforce federal privacy and data protection regulations. The FTC has taken the position that deceptive practices include a company`s failure to comply with its published privacy promises and its failure to provide adequate security of personal information, in addition to its use of deceptive advertising or marketing methods. Other federal status primarily address specific sectors, such as financial services and healthcare. In parallel to the federal regime, state level statutes often differ considerably from one state to another, and some are comprehensive, while other cover areas as diverse as protecting library records to keeping homeowners free from drone surveillance. Although there is no general federal legislation impacting data protection, there are a number of federal data protection laws that are sector-specific or focus on particular types of data. By way of example, the Driver's Privacy Protection Act of 1994 (DPPA)[18] governs the privacy and disclosure of personal information gathered by state Departments of Motor Vehicles. Children's information is protected at the federal level under the Children's Online Privacy Protection Act (COPPA)[19] which prohibits the collection of any information from a child under the age of 13 online and from digitally connected devices, and requires publication of privacy notices and collection of verifiable parental consent when information from children is being collected. The Video Privacy Protection Act (VPPA)[20] restricts the disclosure of rental or sale records of videos or similar audio-visual materials, including online streaming. Similarly, the Cable Communications Policy Act of 1984 includes provisions dedicated to the protection of subscriber privacy. State laws also may impose restrictions and obligations on businesses relating to the collection, use, disclosure, security, or retention of special categories of information, such as biometric data, medical records, SSNs, driver's licence information, email addresses, library records, television viewing habits, financial records, tax records, insurance information, criminal justice information, phone records, and education records, just to name some of the most common. Every state has adopted data breach notification legislation that applies to certain types of personal information about its residents. Even if a business does not have a physical presence in a particular state, it typically must comply with the state's laws when faced with the unauthorised access to, or acquisition of, personal information it collects, holds, transfers or processes about that state's residents. The types of information subject to these laws vary, with most states defining personal information to include an individual's first name or first initial and last name, together with a data point including the individual's SSN, driver's licence or state identification card number, financial account number or payment card information. Some states are more active than others when it comes to data protection. Massachusetts, for example, has strong data protection regulations, requiring any entity that receives, stores, maintains, processes, or otherwise has access to "personal information" of a Massachusetts resident in connection with the provision of goods or services, or in connection with employment:

- to implement and maintain a comprehensive written information security plan (WISP) addressing 10 core standards
- to establish and maintain a formal information security programme that satisfies eight core requirements, which range from encryption to information security training.

In 2019, New York expanded its data breach notification law to include the express requirement that entities develop, implement and maintain "reasonable" safeguards to protect the security, confidentiality and integrity of private information. Significantly, New York's SHIELD Act[21] identifies a series of administrative, technical, and physical safeguards which, if implemented, are deemed to satisfy New York's reasonableness standard under the law. Previously, New York prioritised the regulation of certain financial institutions doing business in the state, by setting minimum cybersecurity standards, with requirements for companies to perform periodic risk assessments and file annual compliance certifications. Illinois has a uniquely expansive state law, which imposes requirements on businesses that collect or otherwise obtain biometric information. The Illinois Biometric Information Privacy Act (BIPA)[22] is notable as, at the time of writing, the only state law regulating biometric data usage that allows private individuals to sue and recover damage for violations. More recently, we have seen a number of states push towards enacting comprehensive consumer data privacy laws. Specifically, in 2020, California amended the CCPA with the California Privacy Rights Act (CPRA)[23], which expanded the rights granted to consumers and increased compliance obligations on businesses. In 2021, Virginia enacted the Consumer Data Protection Act (CDPA)[24] becoming the second state with a comprehensive data privacy law, followed shortly thereafter by Colorado, which enacted the Colorado Privacy Act (CPA)[25]. Continuing this trend, in March 2022,Utah enacted the Utah Consumer Privacy Act (UCPA)[26], and in May 2022, Connecticut enacted an Act Concerning Personal Data Privacy and Online Monitoring (Connecticut Privacy Act), bringing the number of US states with comprehensive data privacy legislation up to five. These recently passed state date privacy laws are not yet effective. California and Virginia coming into effect on January 1, 2023, followed by the Colorado and Connecticut on July 1,2023 and Utah on December 31, 2023. In the absence of a data privacy framework at the federal level, states continue to pursue legislation. At the time of writing, the authors are aware of 13 comprehensive privacy bills before the legislatures of eight different states. Key sector-specific laws include those covering financial services, healthcare, telecommunications, and education. The Gramm

Leach Bliley Act (GLBA)[27] governs the protection of personal information in the hands of banks, insurance companies and other companies in the financial service industry. This statute addresses "Non-Public Personal Information" (NPI), which includes any information that a financial service company collects from its customers in connection with the provision of its services. It imposes requirements on financial service industry companies for securing NPI, restricting disclosure and use of NPI and notifying customers when NPI is improperly exposed to unauthorised persons. The Fair Credit Reporting Act (FCRA)[28], as amended by the Fair and Accurate Credit Transactions Act (FACTA)[29], restricts use of information with a bearing on an individual's creditworthiness, credit standing, credit capacity, character, general reputation, personal characteristics or mode of living to determine eligibility for credit, employment or insurance. It also requires the truncation of credit card numbers on printed receipts, requires the secure destruction of certain types of personal information, and regulates the use of certain types of information received from affiliated companies for marketing purposes. In addition to financial industry laws and regulation, the major credit card companies require businesses that process, store or transmit payment card data to comply with the Payment Card Industry Data Security Standard (PCI-DSS)[30].The Health Information Portability and Accountability Act, as amended (HIPAA)[31] protects information held by a covered entity that concerns health status, provision of healthcare or payment for healthcare that can be linked to an individual. Its Privacy Rule regulates the collection and disclosure of such information. Its Security Rule imposes requirements for securing this data. The Telephone Consumer Protection Act (TCPA)[32] and associated regulations regulate calls and text messages to mobile phones, and regulate calls to residential phones that are made for marketing purposes or using automated dialling systems or pre-recorded messages.

While the United States has no plenary data protection

regulator, the FTC's authority is very broad, and often sets the tone on federal privacy and data security issues. In addition, a variety of other agencies regulate data protection through sectoral laws, including the Office of the Comptroller of the Currency (OCC), the Department of Health and Human Services (HHS), the Federal Communications Commission (FCC), the Securities and Exchange Commission, the Consumer Financial Protection Bureau (CFPB) and the Department of Commerce.

There are some key principles that apply into processing personal date in the USA:

- Transparency: The FTC has issued guidelines espousing the principle of transparency, recommending that businesses: (i) provide clearer, shorter, and more standardised privacy notices that enable consumers to better comprehend privacy practices;(ii) provide reasonable access to the consumer data they maintain that is proportionate to the sensitivity of the data and the nature of its use; and (iii) expand efforts to educate consumers about commercial data privacy practices.
- Lawful basis for processing: While there is no "lawful basis for processing" requirement under U.S. law, the FTC recommends that businesses provide notice to consumers of their data collection, use and sharing practices and obtain consent in limited circumstances where the use of consumer data is materially different than claimed when the data was collected, or where sensitive data is collected for certain purposes.
- Purpose limitation: The FTC recommends privacy-by-design practices that include limiting "data collection to that which is consistent with the context of a particular transaction or the consumer's relationship with the business, or as required or specifically authorized by law".
- Retention: The FTC recommends privacy-by-design practices that implement "reasonable restrictions on the retention of data", including disposal "once the data has

outlived the legitimate purpose for which it was collected".

Also there are some key rights that individuals have in relation to processing of their personal data:

- Right of access to data/copies of data: These rights are statute-specific. For example, under certain circumstances, employees are entitled to receive copies of data held by employers. In other circumstances, parents are entitled to receive copies of information collected online from their children under the age of 13. Under HIPAA, individuals are entitled to request copies of medical information held by a health services provider. At the state level, the CCPA provides a right of access for California residents to personal information held by a business relating to that resident. The CPRA, Virginia CDPA, the Colorado Privacy Act the Utah Consumer Privacy Act, and the Connecticut Privacy Act will provide a similar right.
- Right to rectification of errors: These rights are statute-specific. Some laws, such as the FCRA, provide consumers with a right to review data about the consumer held by an entity and request corrections to errors in that data. At the state level, the right to correct information commonly attaches to credit reports, as well as criminal justice information, employment records, and medical records. Upcoming state data privacy legislation, including the CPRA, the Virginia CDPA, the Colorado Privacy Act, and the Connecticut Privacy Act provide a consumer right to correct inaccuracies in personal data held by a business.
- Right to deletion/right to be forgotten: These rights are statute-specific. By way of federal law example, COPPA provides parents the right to review and delete their children's information and may require that data be deleted even in the absence of a request. Some state laws, such as the CCPA, provide a right of deletion for residents of the respective states, with certain exceptions. The CPRA, Virginia CDPA, the Colorado Privacy Act, the Utah

Consumer Privacy Act, and the Connecticut Privacy Act will provide a similar right to delete.

- Right to object to processing: These rights are statute-specific. Individuals are given the right to opt out of receiving commercial (advertising) email sunder CAN-SPAM and the right to not receive certain types of calls to residential or mobile telephone numbers without express consent under the TCPA. Some states provide individuals with the right not to have telephone calls recorded without either consent of all parties to the call or consent of one party to the call.

- Right to restrict processing: These rights are statute-specific. Certain laws restrict how an entity may process consumer data. For example, the CCPA allows California residents, and the Nevada Privacy Law allows Nevada residents to prohibit a business from selling that individual's personal information. The newly enacted Virginia CDPA, Colorado Privacy Act, and Connecticut Privacy Act will provide a right to restrict processing for the purposes of sale, targeted advertising, and profiling. The Utah Consumer Privacy Act will provide a slightly narrower right to restrict processing for the purposes of sale or targeted advertising.

- Right to object to marketing: These rights are statute-specific. Several laws permit consumers to restrict marketing activities involving their personal data. Under CAN-SPAM, for example, individuals may opt out of receiving commercial (advertising) emails. Under the TCPA, individuals must provide express written consent to receive marketing calls/texts to mobile telephone lines. California's Shine the Light Act requires companies that share personal information for the recipient's direct marketing purposes to either provide an opt-out or make certain disclosures to the consumer of what information is shared, and with whom. The CPRA, Virginia CDPA, the Colorado Privacy Act, the Utah Consumer Privacy Act, and the Connecticut Privacy Act will provide consumers with the right to opt out of processing of their personal information for targeted advertising.

- Right to complain to the relevant data protection authority: These rights are statute-specific. By way of example, individuals may report unwanted or deceptive commercial email("spam") directly to the FTC, and telemarketing violations directly to the FCC. Similarly, anyone may fi le a HIPA a complaint directly with the Department of Health and Human Services (HHS). At the state level, California residents may report alleged violations of the CCPA to the California Attorney General. Under the CPRA, California residents will be able to report alleged violations to the CPPA. Similarly, under the UCPA, Utah residents will be able to report alleged violations to the state's Consumer Protection Division.

Instead in Europe is going to be much easier to categorized all the organizations and the following law, all member states will take part in the EU regulations.

# 2.2 EUROPEAN CYBERSECURITY ORGANIZATION

The rapid increasing of cybersecurity attacks and challenges in the last years has forced the all world to devise new mandatory regulations. The objectives of these requirements are to help combat cybercrime by increasing organizations' level of response and cybersecurity capabilities. It is fundamental to constantly keep track of updated cybersecurity laws and information security standards can be very difficult and time consuming for experts in cybersecurity. Very often is overlooked, or expert are forced to prioritize local regulation news. In the European union cybersecurity regulations have a great impact in organizations, companies and institutions, especially for the financial and healthcare industries.

The end of the second decade of the 21st century has been the best of times for EU's cybersecurity law and policy: Its NIS Directive has been transposed into all Member States' national law, creating a new administrative structure at EU and Member State level and mandating relevant policies and strategies to update and harmonise those that were already in place. Its Cybersecurity Act[33] of 2019 incorporated the EU Agency for Cybersecurity (ENISA), and promises to install a new European cybersecurity certification scheme. To support policy with funding, large sums of research money have been spent on the development of cybersecurity tools and the relevant framework. However, EU's significant regulatory activity is faced with substantial difficulties. While cybersecurity concerns are placed high on the list of issues that worry Europeans making a regulatory response pressing, the cybersecurity theoretical framework is far from concluded: Difficulties start as early as when attempting to define the term, ultimately divulging a lack of common understanding. Different actors understand cybersecurity differently under different circumstances. A distinction that could perhaps prove useful in creating clarity as to its exact meaning would distinguish between cybersecurity as praxis and cybersecurity as a state. Cybersecurity as praxis would then be understood as the activities and measures that need to be undertaken in order to accomplish cybersecurity's aims and objectives. Accordingly, cybersecurity as a state would mean the condition that is achieved once cybersecurity as praxis has succeeded; Within cybersecurity as a state persons need to be protected against any cyber threat. A distinction between cybersecurity as praxis and cybersecurity as a state would not only be useful in delineating the term's content but could also constitute the necessary theoretical groundwork for development, ultimately, of a new right to cybersecurity. EU law has already taken positive steps towards acknowledgement of a new right to cybersecurity. However, a lot more needs to be done; Past progress needs to be continued and updated. A conceivable next step could take the form of formal acknowledgement of such a new right in EU law, in a future amendment of the Act's provisions or otherwise. EU's significant regulatory activity is faced with substantial difficulties. On the one hand, cybersecurity concerns are placed high in the list of issues that worry Europeans. This makes regulatory response pressing. On the other hand, the cybersecurity theoretical framework is far from concluded. Difficulties start as early as when attempting to even define the term: the many contexts and approaches to cybersecurity as well as the fact that its origins are traced in literature rather than specialised documentation, make it impossible to reach a generally agreed upon definition. This has led to definitional approaches that vary considerably, from acknowledging the impossibility of the task and questioning the very need for a definition, to providing complex and comprehensive wording that is more akin to a concept than a single term. Definitional difficulties ultimately divulge a lack of common understanding. Different actors understand cybersecurity differently under different circumstances. A distinction that could perhaps shed some new light and create clarity as to its exact meaning would distinguish between cybersecurity as praxis and cybersecurity as a state. Cybersecurity as praxis would then be understood as the activities and measures to accomplish cybersecurity's aims and objectives. It would include a requirement to act, to undertake concrete actions. Accordingly, cybersecurity as a state would mean the condition that is achieved once cybersecurity as praxis has succeeded; within cybersecurity as a state natural and legal persons need to be protected against any cyber threat. Within its protective sphere natural and legal persons need to be secure, to have a claim to remain so and for others to respect their wish. A distinction between cybersecurity as praxis and cybersecurity as a state would not only be useful in delineating the term's content but could also constitute the necessary theoretical groundwork for development, ultimately, of a new right to cybersecurity. A new right to cybersecurity would allow natural and legal persons to defend themselves against cyber threats. It would place obligations upon all other parties to respect it, and, if applicable, take concrete actions in this regard. If a state of cybersecurity is to be achieved in EU law, a new right to cybersecurity is the suitable legal tool to create and defend it. EU law has already taken positive steps towards acknowledgement of a new right to cybersecurity. Definite progress towards this direction may be viewed if the texts and the approaches of the NIS Directive and the EU Cybersecurity Act are put to comparison. The latter, although in a cautious and minimalistic manner, has taken important steps and made significant contributions towards identifying the basic components of a new right: the cybersecurity addressees and recipients, as well as, its subject-matter and scope. However, a lot more needs to be done; past progress needs to be continued and updated. A conceivable next step could take the form of formal acknowledgement of such a new right in EU law, in a future amendment of the Act's provisions, or otherwise. It is suggested that this could be achieved through distinction between cybersecurity as praxis, whereby actions and measures undertaken by the cybersecurity addressees are meant, and cybersecurity as a state, whereby a conceptual protective sphere is created to the benefit of the cybersecurity recipients within which they are and remain secure. This distinction is considered useful in order to create clarity and improve understanding in today's complex global environment that creates confusion. Such confusion becomes evident as early as when trying to provide cybersecurity with a commonly accepted definition. The distinction between cybersecurity as praxis and as a state is also critical while examining existence of a new right to cybersecurity, because it sheds light into its necessary component parts: under a praxis lens the cybersecurity's addressees, recipients, as well as, its subject-matter and protective scope become identifiable; under a state lens, the cybersecurity protected sphere for natural and legal persons emerges, that in fact forms the core of the right to cybersecurity. A generally agreed upon definition for cybersecurity seems today more elusive than ever. This is reflected not only in the numerous definitions to be found in formal texts of various aims, contexts and statuses, but also in an increase in recent years of academic contributions that are aimed exactly at addressing this problem. Nevertheless, in order to establish existence of a right to cybersecurity in EU law definitional clarity is of the essence. A right requires a well-described content that remains at all times identifiable both by its recipients and by its addressees. An "enveloping term" or even acceptance that a definition for cybersecurity is not necessary threatens to blur its scope and objectives and to create confusion as to its exact particulars. Dictionaries define "cybersecurity" as "measures taken to protect a computer or computer system against unauthorized access or attack" or "things that are done to protect a person, organization, or country and their computer information against crime or attacks carried out using the internet" or "the state of being protected against the criminal or unauthorized use of electronic data, or the measures taken to achieve this". Encyclopaedias[34], however, place emphasis on "protection" per se. In Britannica there is no "cybersecurity" term; instead, only "computer security" is listed "the protection of computer systems and information from harm, theft, and unauthorized use". Similarly, Wikipedia considers "cybersecurity", "computer security" and "information technology security" as synonyms: "the protection of computer systems from the theft of or damage to their hardware, software, or electronic data, as well as from the disruption or misdirection of the services they provide". Consequently, in this case definitions for cybersecurity move decidedly from "things that are done to protect" or "a state of being protected" to "protection of computer systems", therefore to the aims of cybersecurity. Indeed, describing its aims seems the preferred way to define cybersecurity today. In the words of Singer and Friedman, "the canonical goals of security in an information environment result from this notion of a cyberthreat. Traditionally, there are three goals: Confidentiality, Integrity, Availability, sometimes called the "CIA triad". The CIA triad denotes any and all actions that are aimed at creating and preserving the confidentiality, integrity and availability of the underlying information technology asset. The CIA triad, that originated from a combination of academic papers and expert reports, was widely adopted and finally found its way into EU law, that also added to the triad the concepts of resilience and authenticity. The formal definition of cybersecurity, however, in EU law is found in the text of the EU Cybersecurity Act: "cybersecurity means the activities necessary to protect network and information systems, the users of such systems, and other persons affected by cyber threats". A noteworthy definitional approach to cybersecurity comes from the CEN single bond CENELEC Focus Group on Cybersecurity[35], created by the European Standardization Organizations CEN, CENELEC and ETSI in 2011, that released a report in 201619 in response to EU's Cybersecurity Strategy. The report approached the term from a more technical than conceptual point of view, focusing on cataloguing threats and risks. Its recommendation is that there is no need for a definition of cybersecurity, at least "not in the conventional sense that we tend to apply to definitions for simple things like authentication of an identity. The problem is that cybersecurity is an enveloping term and it is not possible to make a definition to cover the extent of cybersecurity coverage". Instead, "a contextual definition is relevant, fits and is already in use". This approach, under the exact same wording, had been earlier also suggested by ENISA, which had anyway taken active part in the above standardisation work. In legal theory, Schatz, Bashroush and Wall have applied a computational approach to define cybersecurity as "the approach and actions associated with security risk management processes followed by organizations and states to protect confidentiality, integrity and availability of data and assets used in cyber space. The concept includes guidelines, policies and collections of safeguards, technologies, tools and training to provide the best protection for the state of the cyber environment and its users." Their result, while successful in identifying the common denominator, has provided, however, a text akin more to a concept than a definition. Similarly, Fuster and Jasmontaite found that "the term 'cybersecurity', from an EU perspective, entails a combination of cyber resilience, cybercrime, cyber defence, (strictly) cybersecurity and global cyberspace issues". In addition to the above, many authors consider controlling user actions (through training or security control) as a core element of cybersecurity. These attempts in essence illustrate the definitional impasse and perhaps justify the ENISA and CENELEC view that a definition for cybersecurity, it being an "enveloping term", may not be necessary because it is impossible. In Odermatt's words[36], "without a clear definition of cybersecurity and its key terms, it is difficult for the EU to establish a comprehensive vision". A definition does not only warrant a standard way of reference but also helps to shed light onto the defined term. The list of definitions above already demonstrates basic differences in perspective: to some cybersecurity denotes measures and actions, to others a state of being protected, to others an ability to resist, and, to those adhering to the CIA triad, a set of aims and purposes. These are fundamentally different approaches. Notwithstanding the fact that professionals and theorists (information technology specialists, lawyers, social scientists, philosophers) may attach their own specific content onto cybersecurity, it is of fundamental importance to be clear on such basic distinctions as to whether cybersecurity is a set of actions, a state or both. This distinction will be elaborated in detail in the subsections that immediately follow. Cybersecurity as praxis includes all actions and measures undertaken by the cybersecurity addressees in order to achieve the cybersecurity aims. Praxis therefore includes actionable items: originating from that set of cybersecurity definitions examined above that are based on "measures taken to protect" or "things that are done", cybersecurity as praxis denotes acts to serve a purpose. These acts are carried out by the cybersecurity addressees, the designated actors in cybersecurity rules and regulations. The aims of cybersecurity are set each time in the respective regulatory documents and may differ amongst them including anything from the confidentiality, integrity and availability of data and services to a more general approach such as the one adopted in the EU Cybersecurity Act against "cyber threats". The measures and actions to achieve them may include processes, organisational measures taken in the natural or the digital world, the implementation of security software systems etc. Because cybersecurity as praxis is very much dependant on an underlying information technology asset, which at times may constitute the main consideration for those involved in providing it, it is considered important to clarify cybersecurity's theoretical basis and components. The topic as practiced today being highly specialist and technical, and given also the above definitional divergences, an analysis of its theoretical constituting parts is believed to benefit all stakeholders. Closer examination of the cybersecurity addressees and recipients as well as of its subject-matter and scope is believed to be critical not only in creating better understanding on the exact content of cybersecurity but also in providing sound theoretical groundwork to those involved in providing it. Cybersecurity as praxis could conceptually either include everybody or pertain only to a few. Under a participatory approach everybody would somehow need to act or carry out measures: individuals and legal persons would have to take action, as prescribed by law or other regulations, in order for each to contribute proportionately to achieving the cybersecurity aims. For example, organisations would need to implement technical and organisational measures and individuals would have to apply so-called "cyber hygiene" practices. Altogether, these collective measures would be aimed to serve the cybersecurity aims. Such an all-encompassing model would in effect resemble real-world security practice, whereby every organisation needs to take security-related measures and individuals need to lock their doors. Conversely, under a restrictive approach only a few designated actors would be the cybersecurity addressees. Under this approach cybersecurity as praxis would not be addressed to everyone but would rather be a closed matter. Concrete actions would need to be taken by the designated few, who for some reason have been singled out and for whom a policy decision has been made that they are the only ones that need to act. For example, cybersecurity as praxis could be addressed only to a few organisations, that would need to apply technical and organisational measures. As regards the cybersecurity recipients here again an all-encompassing policy option would mean that everybody has an expectation to cybersecurity while a restrictive policy would limit the cybersecurity recipients to only a few. The exact content of such an expectation to cybersecurity will be elaborated in the subsection that immediately follows, where cybersecurity as a state will be discussed. Here it is enough to be noted that, while legislators and policymakers are of course free to decide, the nature of cybersecurity as a state and its broad connection to security most likely prejudice its circle of recipients. In other words, everybody who is active digitally, natural and legal persons alike, should be considered a cybersecurity recipient. The expectation to a state of cybersecurity cannot justifiably be confined to a closed set of natural or legal persons. Finally, as regards its subject-matter and protective scope, the question here is what cybersecurity as praxis actually protects. "Network and information systems" cannot be the subject-matter of cybersecurity. The protection of a computer system cannot be an end in itself. A "network and information system" is essentially hardware, a tangible system composed of microchips, hard drives, cables, etc. As such it is similar to an equally complex tangible system such as a car, a plane or a bank safe. Although a multitude of laws and regulations are in place prescribing how to manufacture a car or a plane or a bank money safe, neither the car, nor the plane or the money safe are the ultimate objects of protection of these laws: It is passengers or money . In other words, the hardware is the means through which to access the data, not an end in itself. Data, being the tangible target of cyber threats, easily pass the threshold of hardware as a means to a purpose discussed above. However, legal systems do not protect property as an end in itself: property is invariably protected in relation to its owner. In the above example of the bank money safe the equivalent would be that money is the recipient of all rules and regulations of bank law. This, of course, is not the case. In fact, it is the protection of the economy, as a basic societal component, that is the actual subject-matter of the relevant laws. Similarly, in the case of data, although they are protected within a cybersecurity context, it is persons having a right or a connection with them that are ultimately protected. Natural and legal persons are therefore the subject-matter of cybersecurity as praxis. They occupy its protective scope. It is to their benefit that cybersecurity addressees are called to act. If cybersecurity as praxis achieves its aims, it will be natural and legal persons that will be in the position to feel this security, to confirm that cybersecurity as praxis has succeeded. Persons are the recipients of cybersecurity as praxis, they are the ones to the benefit of which others have to act. Having established the theoretical groundwork for cybersecurity as praxis, a clear distinction needs to be made with actual cybersecurity practice today. As it will be later demonstrated, the topic has developed, both from a technical and a legal perspective, into a highly technical one focused on IT assets and infrastructures. This is a development that is most likely consistent with the early stages of cyberattacks and cybercrime, when cybersecurity threats and attacks were expectedly placed on expensive or important targets that promised maximum return. Therefore, from this point of view actual practice has perhaps blurred the greater cybersecurity picture, drawing attention away from its actual subject-matter and protective scope. Nevertheless, once cyberattacks have entered the mainstream, as is perhaps gradually becoming the case today, then cybersecurity will need to become universally applicable to all people and all systems in the same manner as a general right to security forms today an integral part of their everyday lives. Cybersecurity as a state is met when cybersecurity as praxis has achieved its purposes. In other words, if cybersecurity as praxis has achieved its protective scope, a state of cybersecurity ensues for the cybersecurity recipients. Once within this protective sphere of cybersecurity, natural and legal persons may enjoy a state of cybersecurity, having the expectation that they are, and remain, cybersecure. Or, it is a sphere within which protection is afforded to natural and legal persons from cyber threats, either present or potential. The state of cybersecurity is of course a theoretical construct. It can be imagined as a sphere of protection within which the recipients of cybersecurity are allowed to enjoy unhindered a condition of cybersecurity. Within it, their data and themselves are protected against any cyber threats. Each recipient of cybersecurity has full control over its own respective sphere: it can, or should, take measures to protect it. Third parties need to respect and comply with its will. However, being a theoretical construct, a state of cybersecurity does not necessarily include a successful attainment of its aims and purposes. It is at this point where the "ability to protect or defend", as identified in US cybersecurity standards, proves useful. An "ability to protect or defend" assumes a protective sphere, something to actually protect or defend. This protective sphere needs to have boundaries that are distinguishable to its recipient and to third parties. In addition, an "ability to protect or defend" includes both a will and the means to do so. If the will is taken for granted within a state of cybersecurity, the means through which to accomplish this need to be better approached. Legal means would unavoidably involve a right to enjoy a state of cybersecurity and an obligation of third parties to respect it. Organisational/technical means involve protective techniques and procedures. However, these measures are different than the ones implemented at the stage of cybersecurity as praxis. During the praxis stage the cybersecurity addressees needed to act in order to create a protective sphere. Once cybersecurity as a state has been created, the same or additional addressees need to take the same or a different set of actions in order to preserve it. Acknowledgement of a state of cybersecurity unavoidably affects both the cybersecurity addressees and the cybersecurity recipients. Although a state of cybersecurity could well be the result of actions of a few while everybody else merely keeps an expectation for them to act, once cybersecurity as a state has been achieved its preservation may no longer burden only the few that helped create it. In other words, policy choices during the praxis stage do not need to prejudice policy choices once cybersecurity as a state has been created. Far more important, however, is the fact that acknowledgement of a state of cybersecurity is critical in the formulation of a right to cybersecurity. Rights are "entitlements to perform certain actions, or to be in certain states; or entitlements that others perform certain actions or be in certain states". Similarly, the Oxford English Dictionary provides the definition of a right "the state of being entitled to a privilege or immunity or authority to act". While a number of distinctions and categorisations has been suggested by rights' philosophers and legal theorists, common amongst most is a protected sphere placed at the control of the right's recipient: an "immunity" under the Hohfeldian system[37], or a "passive right" under the active and passive rights distinction, or a "negative right" under the positive and negative rights categorisation. Common to all the above is acknowledgement of a state, a normative situation that cannot be affected or altered in any way without the consent of the rightsholder. For the purposes of this analysis, a right to cybersecurity would effectively mean the rightsholders' claim that their state of cybersecurity, as created by cybersecurity as praxis, remains intact by infringements and cyber threats. If one simply removes the "cyber" prefix from the definition given to cybersecurity in the EU Cybersecurity Act the result would read: "security means the activities necessary to protect assets, their users and other persons by threats". This forms a good definitional approach to security: the Cambridge Dictionary defines "security" as "protection of a person, building, organization, or country against threats such as crime or attacks by foreign countries". Consequently, a reasonable assumption would be that cybersecurity is nothing different than real-life security projected onto the digital realm. Or, in other words, that cybersecurity is a subset of security, promising individuals that they will be as secure in the digital world as they are in the real world. Hence, under the same assumption, there would be no need for a new right to cybersecurity because the general right to security is enough. In the real world the individual right to security is a fundamental human right. Human rights' theory suggests that the right to security constitutes a "basic" human right, because it is necessary for other fundamental human rights to be meaningful and even possible. It is therefore claimed to take precedence over other human rights, because its "enjoyment is essential to the enjoyment of all other rights" or "no-one can fully enjoy any right that is supposedly protected by society if someone can credibly threaten him or her with murder, rape, beating, etc., when he or she tries to enjoy the alleged right". However, interpretational difficulties quickly become noticeable: security can be threatened and destroyed by other than human agents, for example natural disasters, foreign states etc. In addition, the right to security can become difficult to clearly distinguish from the equally basic rights to life, liberty and even property. Each one of them may be interpreted not only as a right to be protected but also as a request to be provided with protection. In the words of Lazarus, "for the purposes of clarity, therefore, it makes sense to distinguish at the outset between a justiciable right to security; a non-justiciable right to security that is supported by non-judicial compliance mechanisms; the expression of a human rights standard or aspiration within an institutional context; and the expression of a human rights aspiration within political rhetoric or philosophical discourse. The 'right to security' is expressed in all of these contexts". All these considerations have led in the culmination of a new academic field, namely security studies; security studies approach security as a concept, and not as a fundamental human right alone. This approach echoes ENISA's definitional approach to cybersecurity, that it is impossible to define exactly. Cybersecurity and security would then seem to share the same definitional and contextual difficulties. This finding, however, delineates the relationship between the two: security is not a parent concept to cybersecurity. Instead, the two concepts are independent from each other. Security is a fundamental human right and a concept that finds meaning based on the different contexts it is met. Cybersecurity may lack today the status of a human right, but it too finds meaning depending on the different contexts it is met. The two concepts differ, because security includes real-world circumstances, protecting against real-world threats, while cybersecurity refers to the digital realm, protecting from cyber threats. The two sets of threats do not necessarily coincide. While a time may well be imagined that the real and the digital converge, until such time cybersecurity and security, although sharing the same linguistic root and interpretational difficulties, should be treated as two different concepts and rights, each to be assessed by its own merit. Having established the two facets of cybersecurity, as praxis and as a state, the next step is to apply this distinction to the relevant regulatory approach applied so far in the EU. The aim is to identify the current state of play and to examine how the legislative provisions in effect today justify, or not, a claim for introduction of a new right to cybersecurity in EU law. Recourse, in the sense of a neighbouring model par excellence, will be sought in the field of EU personal data protection law. To-date the EU has enacted two horizontal cybersecurity regulatory instruments, the NIS Directive (that is in the process of being amended through the, sequentially named, NIS 2 Directive) and the EU Cybersecurity Act, and has also established an EU Cybersecurity Agency (ENISA). These basic texts of reference are complemented with numerous case-specific regulations, as well as, a number of cybersecurity provisions to be found in legislative texts of different subject-matter. Non-regulatory instruments adding clarity and case-specific guidance to the field include the work by ENISA and various standards organisations and stakeholders.

In Europe to provide assistance and support to EU member states, business and institutions in the cybersecurity sector and to deliver solutions and improvements to the EU's cybersecurity framework is left to ENSIA (European union agency for cybersecurity). The main role is to promote and support member states, business and EU institutions in dealing with cyber-attacks. ENSIA[38] is replacing the organization " European Union Agency for Network and Information Security" but keeping the same acronym. Unlike its predecessor the new ENISA, thanks to the EU Cybersecurity Act, has been granted a permanent mandate with more power, more resources and new responsibilities. Such us:

- establishing a cybersecurity certification framework for products and services;
- creating and outlining best practices for cybersecurity and laying out steps against ransomware;
- promoting cyber resilience;
- increasing operational cooperation to help EU Member States with handling cybersecurity incidents;
- and supporting the coordination of the EU in case of major cross-border cyberattacks and cybersecurity crises.

These new tasks are based on ENISA's role as secretariat of the national CSIRTs Network that's ensured and encouraged by the NIS Directive[39]. The NIS2 Directive is the EU-wide legislation on cybersecurity[40]. It provides legal measures to boost the overall level of cybersecurity in the EU. The EU cybersecurity rules introduced in 2016 were updated by the NIS2 Directive that came into force in 2023. It modernised the existing legal framework to keep up with increased digitisation and an evolving cybersecurity threat landscape. By expanding the scope of the cybersecurity rules to new sectors and entities, it further improves the resilience and incident response capacities of public and private entities, competent authorities and the EU as a whole. The Directive on measures for a high common level of cybersecurity across the Union provides legal measures to boost the overall level of cybersecurity in the EU by ensuring:

- Member States' preparedness, by requiring them to be appropriately equipped. For example, with a Computer Security Incident Response Team (CSIRT) and a competent national network and information systems (NIS) authority,
- Cooperation among all the Member States, by setting up a Cooperation Group to support and facilitate strategic

cooperation and the exchange of information among Member States.

- A culture of security across sectors that are vital for our economy and society and that rely heavily on ICTs, such as energy, transport, water, banking, financial market infrastructures, healthcare and digital infrastructure.

Businesses identified by the Member States as operators of essential services in the above sectors will have to take appropriate security measures and notify relevant national authorities of serious incidents. Key digital service providers, such as search engines, cloud computing services and online marketplaces, will have to comply with the security and notification requirements under the Directive. The NIS Directive in Article 12 establishes the CSIRTs Network "to contribute to developing confidence and trust between the Member States and to promote swift and effective operational cooperation". The CSIRTs Network is a network composed of EU Member States' appointed CSIRTs and CERT-EU ("CSIRTs Network members"). The European Commission participates in the network as an observer. ENISA is tasked to actively support the CSIRTs cooperation, provide the secretariat and active support for incident coordination upon request. The CSIRTs Network provides a forum where members can cooperate, exchange information and build trust. Members will be able to improve the handling of cross-border incidents and even discuss how to respond in a coordinated manner to specific incidents.

Together with European Commission and ENISA, EE (European Energy) and ISACs (Information Sharing and Analysis Centers) are being closely tied, they work together to develop ISACs on both Eu and national levels, promote new ISACs in new sectors, as well as empower new consortiums that are supervised by the Commission to provide legal and technical support for ISACs. The EE and ISACs are non-profit organizations that operate as information and resource gathering centers, established to aid in thwarting cyber threats. They function as two way

ANTONIO BUHAGIAR

information sharing organizations that provide both the public and private sectors with important news, solutions and utilities on cyber resilience, along with the methods that can be used to strengthen the EU Power Grid`s cyber security.

In 2016 was established another very important self- financed non-profit organization in Belgium named ECSO (European Cyber Security Organization)[41]. With more than 250 members that belong to the cybersecurity industry, it acts as a privileged partner and counterpart of the European Commission in a contractual public-private partnership for cybersecurity. ECSO is recognized within the European institutional landscape, has cross-sectoral partnerships, and federates the European Free Trade Association (EFTA). More importantly, it covers Horizon Europe, a research funding program that plays a big part in funding the EU's cybersecurity resilience. Project with a huge budget (95.5 billion euros) until 2027.

In case of a cybersecurity incidents a group of IT professionals will provide assistance with two groups: Computer Security Incident Response Teams (CSIRTs)[42] and Computer Emergency Response Teams (CERTs)[43], those two will deal with incidents on the spot and cooperate with other CSIRT network to:

- Monitor vulnerable cybersecurity networks and incidents;
- Provide early warnings, alerts, predictions, and announcements about cyber risks;
- Respond to cybersecurity incidents;
- And offer dynamic risk and incident analysis and situational awareness.

Both are implemented under the NIS Directive. It`s mandatory that every EU member state have CSIRT/CERT squads to provide the designated state`s digital communication and telecommunication with cybersecurity coverage.

Even if is main focus is not cybersecurity the Joint Research Center (JRC)[44] of the European Commission is a valuable and active contributor to the field. One major JRC contribution to cybersecurity is the center's work on developing tools like the Cybersecurity Taxonomy. This useful glossary of terminology offers a better overview of the EU's cybersecurity field, including insights, history of attacks and changes, task lists, and more.

# 2.3 CYBERSECURITY REGULATIONS IN THE EUROPEAN UNION

The EU has been actively working on strengthening cybersecurity and the safeguarding of communication and data in multiple fields, including politics, energy, economy, healthcare, and the financial sectors, for quite some time now. These sectors have become increasingly dependent on digital technologies. However, the complex, overlapping legislative systems across these sectors could still prove ineffective for the growing concerns of modern cybersecurity in the future. This, along with the COVID-19 crisis and the ongoing Russia/ Ukraine conflict, has prompted the need for an even more comprehensive cybersecurity regulative framework. In response to these issue the Eu has adopted several regulations such us:

- cybersecurity regulations in the EU;
- cybersecurity policies and guidelines;
- cybersecurity communities;
- compliance resources;
- funding and research programs affecting cybersecurity;
- details with a timeline of legislative changes

A regulation that must be analysed and described is The European General Data Protection Regulation (GDPR)[45]. Introduced and passed in 2016 and in effect as of May 2018, the General Data Protection Regulation (GDPR) is one of the most crucial and far-reaching legislative pieces for organizations operating within the EU. The GDPR's main tasks and obligations concern data privacy, cybersecurity, and breach management. It aims to:

- Standardize data protection regulation in the EU;
- Protect personal data and privacy for EU citizens;
- Simplify regulation processes for international organizations.

Additionally, it aims to encourage controllers and processors to follow relevant protocols, implement data privacy measures, and ensure that data is collected with consent before becoming publicly available. The GDPR applies to all institutions and organizations that handle personal data and operate within the EU and companies that deal business with the EU. Most importantly, financial institutions that handle, control, and process large amounts of data are highly impacted by the GDPR's regulations. The GDPR is one of the world's toughest privacy and data protection laws, yet few organizations completely comply with its statutes. The GDPR generally regulates countries within the European Union and European Economic Area, but its framework has been adopted in many important data privacy laws around the world. Complacency is dangerous territory. Non-compliant entities could be fined up to £18 million or 4% of annual global turnover, it depends which is greater. As of 2018, the Information Commissioner's Office (ICO) enforces GDPR standards. The GDPR updates the 1950 European Convention on Human Rights to make it relevant for the digital age. Article 8 of the convention states that everyone has the right to respect their private family life. In the analog era that birthed the convention, the boundaries between public and private life were bold and easily identified. Today, they're ambiguous and blurred. Without a clear and enforced standard like the GDPR, customers can never be confident that their private data, and therefore their private life, is being respected. According to Article 4 of the GDPR, personal data is defined as any information that relates to an identified or identifiable natural person. In other words, personal data is any data that is linked to the identity of a living person. Personal data is format-agnostic to include images, video, audio, numerals, and words. This doesn't only include direct associations, such as financial information and addresses, but also indirect links, such as evaluations relating to the behaviour patterns of a person. Inaccurate information relating to data subjects is still considered personal data because this information is linked to an identity. If, however, the information is associated with a fictional entity, it's not considered personal data. The GDPR impacts any organization that offers goods and services to people in the EU. This includes entities that are not located in the EU. If you run a business online, you never know for certain whether the people you transact with are located in the EU. For this reason, all online businesses should be GDPR-compliant as a protective measure.

In order to strengthen cybersecurity, the European commission and the High Representative of the Union for Foreign Affairs and Security Policy from European External Action Service (EEAS), at the end of 2020, presented and adopted a new EU Cybersecurity Strategy[46]. As a crucial part of shaping Europe's 'Digital Future,' the conclusions in the EU cybersecurity strategy emphasize the importance of setting key objectives for preserving an open economy while the members countries maintain an autonomous approach in their cybersecurity measures. This new EU Strategy calls for enhancing the cyberspace security of fundamental services across Europe like healthcare, energetics, and infrastructure, as well as the ever-increasing number of devices and networks in homes and properties. The strategy consists of two straightforward legislative proposals for more efficient regulations and policies that address:

- the need for updates of the cybersecurity directive for networks,
- the protection of critical entities.

This digital solutions will put people first by opening up new opportunities for business, encouraging the development of trustworthy technology, foster an open and democratic society, enable a vibrant and sustainable economy and help fighting climate change and achieve the green transition. The strategy put it`s fundamental on three main pillar to ensure that Europe seizes the opportunity and gives its citizens, businesses and governments control over the digital transformation. The three pillar are:

- Technology that work for the people
- A fair and competitive digital economy
- An open, democratic and sustainable society

With this strategy EU will try to aim to become a global role model for the digital economy, support developing economies in going digital and develop digital standards and promote them internationally. This strategy will benefit European citizens by making sure technology improves their daily lives, businesses by empowering them to start, grow, innovate and compete on fair terms and the environment by reaching climate neutrality with the help of digital technologies.

Together with GDPR, the Security of Network and Information Systems Directive (NIS Directive) is the most important segment of non-sector-specific legislation for the finance sector. As of 2022, it has already been implemented by all EU countries as part of the EU Cybersecurity strategy proposed by the European Commission. The NIS Directive was the first ever EU-wide cybersecurity and resilience directive that was made to enhance cybersecurity across the EU and increase cooperation between EU member states on the issue. The NIS Directive laid down tasks and security obligations for operators of essential services (OES). These directives are divided into three crucial parts:

- National capabilities, which require EU member states to have certain cybersecurity means and resources for properly implementing CSIRTs, data protection, IoT and smart infrastructure, cyber threat and risk management,

cyber exercises.
- Cross-border collaboration, which encourages EU countries to collaborate within a designated CSIRT network, as well as other cooperation groups.
- National monitoring of important sectors that forces member states to conduct cybersecurity monitoring of market operators in critical sectors like finance, energy, transport, healthcare, and the overall digital infrastructure, ex-post supervision for important digital service providers.

On the 16th of December 2020 in order to strengthen EU cybersecurity the EC proposed a revised NIS directive called the NIS2, which acts as a new and better replacement for the old 2016 NIS Directive. This new proposal addressed the strengthening of the evolving cyber threat landscape and the ongoing digital transformation galvanized by the COVID-19 crisis. The NIS2 Directive focuses on high-level cybersecurity measures across the European Union. It effectively encourages government bodies in the EU to supervise cybersecurity in their own country while collaborating with other member states. In May 2022, the Council and the European Parliament reached a provisional agreement for the new legislative cybersecurity measures, which calls for stronger risk and incident management and cooperation while widening the rules and regulations that fall within its scope. Given that cybersecurity threats are almost always cross-border, cyberattacks on one country's critical facilities may affect the EU as a whole. NIS2 will set the baseline for cybersecurity risk management measures and reporting obligations across all sectors that are covered by the directive, such as energy, transport, health and digital infrastructure. The revised directive aims to remove divergences in cybersecurity requirements and in implementation of cybersecurity measures in different member states. To achieve this, it sets out minimum rules for a regulatory framework and lays down mechanisms for effective cooperation among relevant authorities in each member state. It updates the list of sectors and activities subject to cybersecurity obligations, and provides for remedies and sanctions to ensure enforcement. The directive will formally establish the European Cyber Crises Liaison Organisation Network (EU-CyCLONe)[47] which will support the coordinated management of large-scale cybersecurity incidents. While under the old NIS directive member states were responsible for determining which entities would meet the criteria to qualify as operators of essential services, the new NIS2 directive introduces a size-cap rule. This means that all medium-sized and large entities operating within the sectors or providing services covered by the directive will fall within its scope. While the agreement between the European Parliament and the Council maintains this general rule, the provisionally agreed text includes additional provisions to ensure proportionality, a higher level of risk management and clear-cut criticality criteria for determining the entities covered. The text also clarifies that the directive will not apply to entities carrying out activities in areas such as defence or national security, public security, law enforcement and the judiciary. Parliaments and central banks are also excluded from the scope. As public administrations are also often targets of cyberattacks, NIS2 will apply to public administration entities at central and regional level. In addition, member states may decide that it applies to such entities at  local level too. To unifies the cybersecurity into a single framework in June 2019 was introduced the Cybersecurity Act. This strengthens the role of ENISA by giving the agency a permanent mandate and more financial and human resources. This means that ENISA can now contribute in operational cooperation and crisis management across the EU with an EU-wide certification scheme that will build trust, increase the growth of the cybersecurity market and ease trade across the EU. ENISA will have a key role in setting up and maintaining the European cybersecurity certification framework by preparing the technical ground for specific certification schemes. It will be in charge of informing the public on the certification schemes and the issued certificates through a dedicated website. ENISA is mandated to increase operational cooperation at EU level, helping EU Member States who wish to request it to handle their cybersecurity incidents, and supporting the coordination of the EU in case of large-scale cross-border cyberattacks and crises. The cybersecurity act make crucial in maintaining high cybersecurity standards to have a cybersecurity certification for Information and Communications Technology (ICT) products, services and process. The EU cybersecurity certification framework has the sole purpose of establishing and maintaining trust and security in cybersecurity products or services. Additionally, this framework aims to lay down the procedures for EU cybersecurity certification schemes that cover those services and products, and it highly impacts the financial sector. With various EU member countries using different cybersecurity certification schemes, this is very hard because there are regulatory barriers and market fragmentation. Thanks to the Cybersecurity Act and the new European cybersecurity certification framework, companies and organizations that are doing business with the EU can benefit from having their ICT products certified only once and recognized across the EU.

The NIS Directive lays down obligations for all Member States to adopt a national strategy on the security of network and information systems, creates new organisations to develop trust and confidence (the NIS Cooperation Group and the CSIRTs network), introduces obligations for Operators of Essential Services and for Digital Service Providers, as well as, lays down obligations for Member States to designate national competent authorities, single points of contact and CSIRTs. The NIS Directive builds on the Cybersecurity Strategy of the European Union issued in 2013 and also, although not directly related to it, on an older Directive on critical infrastructures, that still remains in effect until today. If put under the cybersecurity as praxis and as a state lens, a number of issues could be identified with regard to the NIS Directive's approach: First, as regards the cybersecurity addressees, the NIS Directive adopts a limited-circle policy approach. It is addressed only to a closed number of actors, essentially Digital Service Providers and Operators of Essential Services, as well as, to Member States and the EU itself. These are expected to take specific actions at the cybersecurity as praxis stage, leaving all other stakeholders unaffected. In essence, only a handful of organisations are expected to take any cybersecurity action under the NIS Directive. Its policy option is not to impose a horizontal approach onto EU societies, whereby everybody would have to act in one way or another, but instead to focus on a very limited circle of cybersecurity addressees. Similarly, the NIS Directive makes no reference to any cybersecurity recipients. Its provisions are open-ended, in the sense that they do not, explicitly at least, name any recipients; legal obligations placed upon its addressees are not introduced to the benefit of any specifically-named natural or legal person. They do not create any rights to any third parties. Accordingly, the NIS Directive does not confer any rights or other means of protection to the persons (legal or natural) whose rights will be infringed if its addressees do not perform their legal duties. If cybersecurity as praxis fails because the NIS Directive addressees infringe its provisions, those affected by this infringement are not enabled to act in any manner. Articles 15 and 17 of the NIS Directive[48] merely grant national supervisory authorities with the power to "issue binding instructions" or ask to "remedy failures". As regards the NIS Directive's subject matter and scope, in its own wording "this Directive lays down measures with a view to achieving a high common level of security of network and information systems within the Union so as to improve the functioning of the internal market". Therefore, it is the "functioning of the internal market" upon which the release of the NIS Directive is based and not the protection of natural and legal persons per se. A "high common level of security" is to be achieved but this is not aimed at the benefit of any cybersecurity recipient but in order to "improve the functioning of the internal market". Admitting that it exists for market purposes only, it is doubtful whether the NIS Directive contributes at all to the creation of a cybersecurity state. The fact that the NIS Directive carries no recipients and identifies only the "functioning of the internal market" as its raison d'être may be understood to mean that its aim is not to serve natural and legal persons' rights and interests in any way. Consequently, it would be only through an interpretational attempt that any protective scope other than for financial interests could be derived out of the NIS Directive: security of network and information systems needs to be reached in order to "improve the functioning of the internal market"; public trust (as also identified in the EU Cybersecurity Act) is an integral component to achieving such "improvement" of the internal market, and, in turn, creation of a protective sphere and the establishment of cybersecurity as a state for natural and legal persons helps create such public trust. However, this is the result of an interpretation. Based strictly on its wording, the NIS Directive constitutes a limited-scope legal tool, addressed only to a few actors, making no reference to any recipients and conferring no rights or creating no protection to anybody in the EU. The NIS Directive may be perceived as a technical, open-ended regulatory instrument aimed merely at improving network and information systems' operation so as to improve the market conditions within Europe. Nevertheless, this characterisation would largely defeat its perception in the EU: In the Commission's own words, admittedly retrospectively, "in an effort to better protect citizens online, the Union's first legal act in the field of cybersecurity was adopted in 2016 in the form of Directive (EU) 2016/1148"[49]. If that is actually the mindset behind its release and its public perception, then the NIS Directive needs to be applied under a much broader lens in order to support both cybersecurity as praxis and cybersecurity as a state considerations. Such an interpretation could be supported by the EU's approach on the cybersecurity instrument that followed the NIS Directive's release three years later, the EU

Cybersecurity Act. The EU Cybersecurity Act seems to amend the NIS Directive's shortcomings identified above and makes important contributions to cybersecurity in Europe, but does so in an unassuming manner. If assessed under word-count metrics, the EU Cybersecurity Act's provisions carry little justification to their title: rather than a list of rights and obligations, as would perhaps be the expected content in any legal "act", they constitute instead, first, the constitutional document of EU's Agency for Cybersecurity (ENISA), and, second, the incorporation framework for a European cybersecurity certification scheme. As regards ENISA, the EU Cybersecurity Act is simply the latest addition to its predecessors of 2004 and 2013, that nevertheless did not carry such an attractive title; in fact, the word "cybersecurity" itself was not to be found at all in their text, despite of the fact that it was well-known and used at the time of their respective release. As regards the European cybersecurity certification scheme, the relevant provisions are only aimed at exactly that, the organisation, setup and operation of a new certification scheme in Europe. From this point of view the most pertinent provisions to the broader cybersecurity purposes in the EU Cybersecurity Act are to be found in its Articles 1 and 2, where its subject matter, scope and definitions are provided respectively. Although quite limited in length, the contribution of these few provisions is disproportionately important. As regards its subject matter and scope, the EU Cybersecurity Act is introduced "with a view to ensuring the proper functioning of the internal market while aiming to achieve a high level of cybersecurity, cyber resilience and trust within the Union" (Art. 1.1)[50]. Here too, as was the case in the NIS Directive, the EU's cybersecurity regulatory intervention is based on the "proper functioning of the internal market"; again, market considerations and not the protection of persons is the raison d'être of the EU Cybersecurity Act. Nevertheless, close comparison of Articles 1.1[51] of EU's two cybersecurity legal instruments demonstrates an important qualitative differentiation in the wording of the Cybersecurity

Act: in its case the "proper functioning of the internal market" is to be achieved "while" aiming to achieve cybersecurity, cyber resilience and trust, placing therefore all four on the same level. On the contrary, in the NIS Directive security was to be achieved "so as to improve" the internal market, thus as merely a means to an end. Similarly, the EU Cybersecurity Act provides a definition for cybersecurity in the EU. The boldness of this policy option ought not be overlooked: against formal recommendation by the very agency the Act creates as EU's Agency for Cybersecurity and against all difficulties highlighted in dictionaries, academic papers and technical reports, the Act decidedly defines cybersecurity as "the activities necessary to protect network and information systems, the users of such systems, and other persons affected by cyber threats" (Art. 2.1)[52]. This definition, being included in EU's Cybersecurity Act, from now on constitutes the formal EU approach on this matter; all other texts and understanding in the EU ought to refer to it. Although the Act is not addressed at Member States, by way of indirect application (ENISA being EU's Agency for Cybersecurity and the certification scheme intended to run throughout Europe), it should be expected that they too will follow the Act's definitional approach. Under the cybersecurity as praxis and as a state lens the Act at first sight appears to relate only to the former: cybersecurity is explicitly perceived as "activities". Action is anticipated prima facie when it comes to cybersecurity. A state of cybersecurity is not, expressly at least, acknowledged. However, an important component of the Act's definition is "cyber threats". These are "any potential circumstance, event or action that could damage, disrupt or otherwise adversely impact network and information systems, the users of such systems and other persons" (Art. 2.8)[53]. What is of extreme importance for the purposes of this analysis is that "persons" are used in the Act both in the "cybersecurity" and in the "cyber threat" definitions: persons are to be protected by cyber threats; and, cyber threats is anything that may disrupt or adversely impact a person. Combination of the two amounts to acknowledgement of cybersecurity as a state: a protective cybersecurity sphere created to the benefit of persons, within which they are protected, they cannot be "damaged, disrupted or otherwise adversely impacted". It should also be noted that these persons are not only the users of the relevant network and information systems but, explicitly, all persons indiscriminately – another indication of the EU Cybersecurity Act's intention to acknowledge cybersecurity as a state. Having established that the EU Cybersecurity Act, although in a minimalistic way, has taken important steps towards understanding of cybersecurity in the EU both as praxis and as a state, it is much easier to divulge its contribution as regards cybersecurity's stakeholders. Here too important change is carried out in a subtle manner. As regards the cybersecurity's addressees, while specific reference is made to Operators of Essential Services and Digital Service Providers, as was the case in the NIS Directive, ENISA's mandate is much broader and is in no manner confined only to them. ENISA has the mandate to assist or intervene, as appropriate each time, whenever a matter of cybersecurity arises in the EU, regardless of its origins. Nowhere in the EU Cybersecurity Act's text is it mentioned that only Operators of Essential Services and Digital Service Providers or even Member States or the EU are expected to act. Cybersecurity is treated instead as a global European concern: "increased digitisation and connectivity increase cybersecurity risks, thus making society as a whole more vulnerable to cyber threats and exacerbating the dangers faced by individuals, including vulnerable persons such as children. In order to mitigate those risks, all necessary actions need to be taken to improve cybersecurity in the Union." An important further contribution of the EU Cybersecurity Act is that it moves decidedly away from the CIA paradigm. The cybersecurity aims in the EU are no longer the confidentiality, integrity, authenticity and availability of data and services as was the case under the NIS Directive. Instead, it is the protection of systems, users and persons by cyber threats. At a higher level, its aim is to "achieve a high level of cybersecurity, cyber resilience and trust". This is an important shift of perspective: the EU cybersecurity edifice moves from a technical objective-orientated system to a rights-based approach. The good standing of systems is set aside (or, more accurately, set as a technical, secondary objective within the EU certification scheme also introduced by the same Act), and the general cybersecurity approach is now rights-orientated. Data and services are no longer the EU cybersecurity aims but, instead, the creation of a protective sphere, whereby no "circumstance, event or action" could possibly "damage, disrupt or otherwise adversely impact" systems and, more importantly, persons. This is a further important step taken by the EU Cybersecurity Act towards acknowledgement of a right to cybersecurity in the EU. In 2020 the Commission released its proposal for an amendment of the NIS Directive, to be sequentially named the NIS 2 Directive. Although at the time of drafting this paper the NIS 2 Directive was still under the law-making process, it is already clear from the Commission's text that the NIS 2 aims to expand the NIS Directive and address its shortcomings, taking however (what is most important for the purposes of this paper) the Cybersecurity Act's achievements for granted. Most notably, the NIS 2 draft Proposal employs the Act's definition of "cybersecurity" for its purposes. Consequently, in spite of its technical character, the NIS 2 Directive, once it comes into effect, will also be aimed at protecting not only "network and information systems", but also "the users of such systems, and other persons affected by cyber threats". Similarly, while the NIS Directive's subject matter is to "lay down measures with a view to achieving a high common level of security of network and information systems within the Union so as to improve the functioning of the internal market", the NIS 2 Directive's scope, once it comes into effect, will be far more visionary: "this Directive lays down measures with a view to ensuring a high common level of cybersecurity within the Union", thus expanding its protective scope also to include individuals. Other than the above changes, the Commission's draft proposal is aimed at addressing the identified NIS Directive's shortcomings. In this context, while broadly following its structure, the NIS 2 Directive text is far more extensive than its predecessor, each one of its chapters being specifically aimed at resolving difficulties caused by the NIS Directive. Consequently, its Chapter I switches to "essential" and "important" entities as the NIS 2 Directive's recipients in order to deal with issues caused by its predecessor's categorisations. Chapter II details the requirements of Member States' national cybersecurity strategies, aiming at harmonisation and enhanced consistency, while at EU level improved cooperation and information exchange is intended to be achieved through Chapter III (and the introduction of yet another EU cooperation network). The Cybersecurity risk management and reporting obligations are detailed under an, expansive, Chapter IV, which presumably needs to be read together with Chapter V on (extended) information sharing practices. Finally, Chapter VI focuses on supervision and enforcement – most notably, however, still staying short of awarding any remedies to individuals. At any event, regardless of its final formulation the fact remains that, as far as the purposes of this analysis are concerned, the NIS 2 draft Proposal builds on the EU Cybersecurity Act's, and therefore creates an EU cybersecurity framework that, taking the cybersecurity definition into account, is ultimately aimed at protecting any "person affected by cyber threats". The EU Cybersecurity Act acknowledges and validates in a subtle manner cybersecurity both as praxis and as a state in the EU. Its definition of cybersecurity, applicable throughout the EU from now on, acknowledges both cybersecurity as praxis, in the sense that it includes all "activities necessary to protect" anybody threatened by cyber threats, and cybersecurity as a state, in the sense that all "persons", regardless whether systems' users or not, are entitled to protection from "any potential circumstance, event or action" that could "adversely impact" them in any way. This understanding of cybersecurity brought by the EU Cybersecurity Act constitutes an important step towards protecting the cybersecurity of all natural and legal persons in the EU through introduction of a new right to cybersecurity. To the extent that this signals an intentional process by the EU legislator, as demonstrated by the evolution from the more technical NIS Directive to the aforementioned definition of cybersecurity in the EU Cybersecurity Act and the visionary aim-setting of the NIS 2 draft Proposal, it is important that law-making efforts continue at least in the same pace, if not escalate. Shortcomings of the current EU regulatory framework on cybersecurity, particularly in terms of a patchwork, have been well-identified. Despite repeated calls for a release of a comprehensive EU cybersecurity regulatory framework (in the form of an EU Cybersecurity Law), this aim remains until today elusive: the EU Cybersecurity Act for the moment stays short of serving this purpose due to its predominantly functional character (being focused for most of its part on ENISA and the certification framework), while other cybersecurity-relevant legal provisions are found scattered in a multitude of legal documents of various legal statuses. Nevertheless, taking for granted the positive steps undertaken by the EU Cybersecurity Act already, the next conceivable stage for EU policy-making would be the formal acknowledgement of a right to cybersecurity. Such a right would be placed at the centre of the emerging EU Cybersecurity Law. A number of reasons justifies the need for introduction of a, new, right to cybersecurity in EU law. First and foremost, despite of the fact that, as seen, cybersecurity as a state is acknowledged in the text of the EU Cybersecurity Act, individuals are not afforded with any legal means with which to protect it. The Act recognises a need to protect all "persons" against any "event or action" that could "damage, disrupt or otherwise adversely impact" them. In order to achieve this, all "activities necessary" need to be carried out, under a cybersecurity as praxis perspective. Admittedly, if a cybersecurity threat is realised and, as a consequence, natural and legal persons are "adversely impacted", it is most likely that other fields of law will apply to a lesser or greater extent, that afford protection to the persons concerned. If, for example, personal data are unlawfully accessed then the European Data Protection Regulation will step in. If proprietary data are unlawfully used, then Intellectual Property Law may provide protection to the natural and legal persons concerned. Unfair competition, civil or even criminal law could also, under certain conditions, step into the picture. However, these legal safeguards are beyond the point of cybersecurity, both from the perspective of its addressees and from the viewpoint of its recipients. For cybersecurity addressees there is an issue of relevance: cybersecurity has been singled out as a separate and important policy field within the EU; a lot of resources and effort have been given into realising a comprehensive policy; specialised administrative mechanisms have been installed both at EU and at Member State level: in the words of Wessel R A, "cybersecurity forms an excellent example of an area in which the different policy fields of the Union need to be combined, and where measures need to be taken at the level of both the EU and the Member States. If no consequences are attached to default or negligence by its addressees, then a very concrete risk is raised that all these efforts do not develop their potential to the fullest extent possible. Good regulation requires consequences to be attached to infringements of obligations. Otherwise, if addressees are not faced with concrete consequences, they may be tempted to be lax on their implementation of the EU cybersecurity requirements, in view of the costs and effort involved. From the cybersecurity recipients' perspective, whether other fields of law protect them anyway is irrelevant. A policy introduced to their benefit, specifically aimed at not damaging, disrupting or adversely impacting them in any way, cannot be applied without their awareness and in their absence. If left in its current wording, as set in the EU Cybersecurity Act, cybersecurity would be a remote concern to be exclusively handled within EU and Member State organisations, essentially a behind-closed-doors policy. Although important in its own merit, such a policy would fail to develop the impact aimed at individual level and would most likely fail to achieve "trust within the Union". Consequently, a right to cybersecurity needs to be formally introduced in EU law as a means of empowering individuals in the digital realm. Individuals need to be able to protect themselves from digital threats. Digital threats consistently occupy the highest places in the lists of concerns raised by individuals today. They therefore need to be provided with the legal means to protect themselves by cyberthreats. This task should not be outsourced exclusively to their governments and the EU; each one needs to become aware of the threat and be afforded with the legal means to make sure that he or she is not "damaged, disrupted or otherwise adversely impacted" by it. A new right to cybersecurity would also induce so-called cyber-hygiene practices: in the same manner that individuals have learned to lock their doors and bicycles in real-life, participating thus in the creation of security for them, they also need to take measures to defend themselves in the digital realm, as assisted by the law. The law-making conditions to introduce a new right to cybersecurity in EU law are already available. As seen, the EU Cybersecurity Act has already paved the way. The basic components for introduction of a new right are already found in its provisions. Any new right would need to create obligations to an indefinite number of addressees and to protect an indefinite number of recipients. The EU Cybersecurity Act has accomplished exactly that: its definition of cybersecurity is open-ended, in the sense that it is neither addressed to a closed circle of actors nor is it restricted in its scope to a small circle of recipients. No longer are critical infrastructures, Operators of Essential Services or Digital Service Providers the only ones that need to act. Instead, anybody ought to undertake "all activities necessary" to protect from cyber threats. Similarly, everybody needs to be protected. The cybersecurity's definition in the Act applies to all persons, not simply the users of the systems under threat. Accordingly, the EU Cybersecurity Act, by moving decidedly away from the CIA paradigm, has shifted towards a rights-based approach. No longer is EU cybersecurity aimed at the good standing of information technology systems, as was the case under the NIS Directive. Through the Act's provisions the aim of EU law is by now the creation of a protective sphere for any person, in which he or she cannot be adversely impacted in any way. In this manner again clear progress in the EU legislator\s mindset is viewable, from the technical premises of the NIS Directive to the ground-setting provisions of the Act, that are subsequently taken for granted by the NIS 2 draft Proposal. Finally, the EU Cybersecurity Act placed on par the functioning of the internal market and the creation of trust in the Union. No longer are diverging cyber strategies by Member States that are distorting the internal market the only reason for release of cybersecurity legislation. Instead, the Act is also aimed to create trust to individuals across the EU. In this way it is not addressed only to organisations and governments but also to persons, who are the recipients of and need to feel such trust. In this manner, because the EU Cybersecurity Act has taken positive steps towards laying down the necessary theoretical groundwork, future introduction of a general right to cybersecurity in EU law has been made possible. A new right to cybersecurity in the EU could, on the one hand, acknowledge an individual's right to defend itself against cyber threats and, on the other hand, place obligations to everyone else to respect it. While the exact contents of such a new right are beyond the scope of this paper, here it is merely noted that such a right could be quite detailed or quite abstract and general. The former would mean that individuals would be afforded with specific rights, special to the cybersecurity conditions and threats, and that the cybersecurity addressees would have to demonstrate compliance by way of concrete actions and measures. The latter would simply acknowledge its existence, and leave it to individuals to remain vigilant and seek redress in front of courts in case of infringement. Finally, the law-making means to introduce a new right to cybersecurity in EU law could, for example, include a relevant amendment of the EU Cybersecurity Act or the NIS (2) Directive in the sense that these are the two obvious candidate legal instruments currently in effect. Alternatively, a right to cybersecurity could be included as a special sub-category of the general right to security in the EU, perhaps by amending Article 6[54] of the EU Charter of Fundamental Rights. Nevertheless, in view of the difficulties in amending fundamental rights' texts and given also the ambitious naming of the EU Cybersecurity Act, it would perhaps be preferable if introduction of a new EU right to cybersecurity was performed through a future amendment of its provisions that could include a third part to cover this topic as well.

EU personal data protection presents stark similarities with cybersecurity. Because they both relate to the digital real they can be considered neighbouring fields. Their shared origins has led to a shared cause: they both aim to protect individuals from risks caused by new technologies. In fact, the GDPR today could be claimed to be the standard EU regulatory mechanism to deal with anything from robots and artificial intelligence to biotechnology, big data or the internet of things. Another common characteristic, perhaps stemming from their relationship with technology, is that they were both developed globally, in a cross-border manner: Dealing essentially with international concerns at state and individual level, they have grown to the task of providing a global regulatory response. Finally, their mode of deployment is similar, in the sense that they both required a new administrative mechanism to be setup in order to serve their purposes. Apart from similarities, cybersecurity and data protection differ most importantly in their scope: data protection has a much more limited scope, aimed only at the protection of personal data. Cybersecurity, on the other hand, is aimed at protecting "persons" against any cyber threat. In spite of personal data occupying a large portion of the digital realm the fact remains that cybersecurity is all-inclusive while data protection is case-specific. The other significant difference refers to time precedence: data protection emerged as early as in the 1970s, while cybersecurity legislation is no older than the early 2000s, despite of the fact that the relevant risks were known at least since the 1980s. This has unavoidably affected the sophistication of each legal system: data protection in the EU is a complex legal system of more than twenty-five years of history and a second-generation text of law, while cybersecurity only got its first specifically-named legal text, the EU Cybersecurity Act, in 2019. However, because of their significant similarities, it is possible that data protection in the EU could serve as a model par excellence for cybersecurity. If this is the case then EU data protection could assist a EU right to cybersecurity in two critical ways: the first refers to its legal basis and the second to EU law's competence to legislate in the cybersecurity field. In order to demonstrate how EU data protection law could assist in these matters attention shall be given to the 1995 EU Data Protection Directive. As far as identification of a suitable legal basis in EU law for development of a new right to cybersecurity is concerned, Article 114 TFEU[55] could well suffice, if at least the EU personal data protection model can be used as evidence. The 1995 EU Data Protection Directive was released on the basis of Article 100a[56] of the Treaty establishing the European Community, whose aim was the "establishment and functioning of the internal market", same as is the case today in the EU Cybersecurity Act. As is known by now, the 1995 EU Data Protection Directive regulated personal data protection in Europe for several years, until the Treaty of Lisbon came in 2008 and explicitly introduced a new right to personal data protection. Consequently, the law-making process in EU law is not necessarily linear. In other words, it is not necessary first for a new right to be spelled out in the Treaties, in order for secondary legislation to further detail its particulars. As has personal data protection demonstrated, a Directive (or, a Regulation, for example the EU Cybersecurity Act) could well grant to Europeans rights and obligations akin to a right, before a right per se finds its way into the Treaties. Developments so far in EU law justify this approach. As seen, there is a clear development towards a more protective scope from the NIS Directive to the EU Cybersecurity Act. The latter, that shares the same legal basis as the 1995 EU Data Protection Directive (now, Article 114 TFEU)[57], could perhaps be amended in the future to include details of a new right to cybersecurity while still within its scope of protection of the "fundamental rights and freedoms" of natural and legal persons. The second case where EU data protection law could substantially assist the birth of a new EU right to cybersecurity refers to addressing the basic question of EU law competence to legislate in the field. The counter-argument in this case is that the EU is limited to introducing legislation to which it has either an exclusive or shared competence, and that cybersecurity falls outside the scope of EU law, being related to public and national security. In the, characteristic, words of Wessel R A, "the fact that the European Union justified and clarified its legal activities in this area in a 110-points preamble to the EU Cybersecurity Act points to an awareness that this is not obvious area to deal with from a legal perspective". Two points can be raised in this regard. First, that cybersecurity is such a broad concept that only parts of it fall outside EU law competence. Topics such as the harmonisation of the Internal Market or protection of the fundamental rights and freedoms of natural and legal persons do fall under EU law competence, and have actually already led to release of the NIS Directive and the EU Cybersecurity Act. While state security and criminal law may lie outside EU law competence, this does not preclude the EU legislator from introducing protective cybersecurity regulatory provisions, akin to a right, to the benefit of Europeans. As discussed above, EU personal data protection shows that the details of a new right may exist in EU law years before its formal acknowledgement in the Treaties. The second point refers to the fact that, again taking EU personal data protection into consideration, fields within and fields outside EU law competence may co-exist under the same regulatory roof. Most notably, this is the case with EU personal data protection today. The 1995 EU Data Protection Directive expressly excluded itself from "public security, defence, state security (including the economic well-being of the state when the processing operation relates to state security matters) and the activities of the state in areas of criminal law". A careful approach as regards state and national security was also maintained under the 2016 EU data protection reform package, despite of EU data protection's newly elevated status as a fundamental individual right: both the GDPR and the LED ultimately excluded from their scope all fields not regulated by EU law. The above approach by EU personal data protection law demonstrates that co-existence under the same fundamental right of fields falling within and fields outside EU law competence is actually possible, under a careful balancing by the EU legislator to accommodate both. Similarly, EU competence to legislate in the cybersecurity field faces the same dilemma and follows the same methodology: Article 1.2[58] of the EU Cybersecurity Act sets that its provisions are "without prejudice to the competences of the Member States regarding activities concerning public security, defence, national security and the activities of the State in areas of criminal law" (Art. 1.2). The NIS Directive kept a cautious stance as well (see its Recital 8). Therefore, it could be claimed that EU cybersecurity is already following the path paved by EU personal data protection, towards eventual introduction of a new right that would at the same time respect EU competences to legislate.

# 2.4 ITALIAN CYBERSECURITY ORGANIZATIONS

Italy made tremendous advances in creating a cybersecurity ecosystem and a new cybersecurity governance/strategy in the belief that a transparent and protected environment can contribute to creating a positive business environment favourable to the birth and development of new companies and to investments in innovation. Innovation is key to the development of a healthy cyber-economy. New investments play a key role in activating a cyber ecosystem, allowing research worldwide to be transformed into business opportunities. In general, a set of organic actions is needed to strengthen existing skills, intercept new talent and create new career paths needed to meet the technological challenges posed by cybersecurity and to improve the relationships between academia and private companies. Joint efforts of all cybersecurity players must aim to build strong and resilient capabilities, particularly in specific sectors of cyberspace. Priority areas to develop cybersecurity know-how are connected to defence and national security issues, critical networks providing essential services to end users and the protection of national businesses. Italian companies are end-users of sophisticated solutions for cyber protection, and at the same time, producers and exporters of advanced technologies, which position Italy among the most important players in the world cyber market. In 2017 and 2018, Italy streamlined and strengthened its cybersecurity structure in order to boost its cyber capabilities.

The Security Intelligence Department (DIS) is at the centre of the Italian cybersecurity ecosystem's governance, acting as[59]:

- Supporting body for the Prime Minister and the Inter-Ministerial Committee for the Security of the Republic (CISR) on cyber issues
- Chair of the Cybersecurity Management Board (NSC), an interagency and intergovernmental operational body within the DIS tasked with cyber crisis prevention, preparation and management
- European Point of Contact under the Network and Information Security (NIS) directive

The NSC is responsible for promoting Italy's participation in cyber activities (such as Cyber Europe organized by ENISA, the European Network and Information Security Agency) and other initiatives aimed at increasing national cybersecurity. NSC also contributed to the creation of the National Laboratory for Artificial Intelligence and Intelligent System and the Italian Industry Plan 4.0 Funding Program launched by the Ministry of Economic Development.

The Joint Command for Cyber Operations (CIOC) was established in 2017 with two main operational objectives: cyber-defence and cyber network-defence. Cyber defence is related to the static defence and protection of critical networks, carried out in coordination with the Ministry of Defence, to ensure their integrity. Cyber network defence is the ability to carry out vulnerability assessments and penetration tests, in order to provide a quick intervention when needed. The CIOC will also contribute to the organization and training of the entire Italian Cybersecurity System.

The Italian strategy provides guidelines for collaboration among both private and public stakeholders, as well as with academia and research. These guideline aim to:

- Strengthen Italian critical infrastructures and other strategic players' defence capabilities;
- Improve cyber actors' technological, operational, and analytic capabilities;
- Boost public-private cooperation;
- Foster cybersecurity culture;
- Support international cooperation.

The main lines of action of the Italian Ministry of Foreign Affairs take into account the complex, interdependent and continuously changing nature of the cyber domain. Therefore, while dedicated to defending Italian communication networks, need also to cooperate in safeguarding a national security perimeter, promoting our research and industrial systems, and engaging in cyber-diplomacy while remaining committed to an accessible, open, interoperable and reliable cyberspace. Italy keeps up its efforts to guarantee the safety and security of cyberspace, the promotion of economic and commercial growth, the protection of human rights and the promotion of fundamental freedoms in cyberspace. To reach these main goals, Italy relies on the importance of international cooperation, and also aims to implement "Confidence Building Measures" among States and shape effective partnerships in promoting security and stability in cyberspace. At the same time, underscore the risks, in particular for those activities that could have a destabilizing effect on international peace and security, including massive denial-of-service attacks, critical infrastructure damage, or other malicious cyber activities that compromise the use and operation of critical infrastructures. Based on this platform, Italy remains committed to playing a pivotal role in many international field, with a view to addressing the major threats in cyberspace. During the G7 Italian presidency in 2017, the so called "Lucca Declaration" was adopted "on Responsible States Behaviour in Cyberspace" although a non-binding statement, it remains an important commitment to tackle "the risk of escalation and retaliation in cyberspace". This same approach has inspired Italy's Chairmanship-in-Office of the OSCE: hosted in Italy in 2018 OSCE-wide Conference on Cyber/ICT Security in Rome, aimed at providing a platform for exchanging views on digital security and highlighting the positive impact that could arise by a full implementation of Confidence Building Measures on transparency, predictability and

International stability. As a member State of both the EU and NATO, Italy supports closer cooperation to promote security and stability in the cyberspace realm.

The Italian national strategy for cybersecurity promotes the integration and a synergistic approach between cyber security companies with different expertise with two main objectives. First, to develop new means and solutions at the national level to tackle cyber challenges. Second, create national "champions" to be able to compete at the highest international level. In this context, the Ministry of Foreign Affairs and International Cooperation, together with other competent institutions, facilitates the development of a cyber supply chain, promoting national and international Business to Business (BtoB), Business to Government (BtoG), and Government to Government (GtoG) cooperation agreements, and contributing to exporting Italian capabilities and strategic know-how globally. Italian Economic Diplomacy is involved in supporting cybersecurity companies that are approaching foreign markets, thanks to the work of the wide network of Embassies and Consulates

around the world. Each year, the Steering Committee for international promotion of Italian companies, co-chaired by the

Minister of Foreign Affairs and International Cooperation and the Minister of Economic Development, sets Italy's priorities for bilateral commercial relations with other Countries. This activity includes the definition of target markets and export sectors, the organization of training activities for entrepreneurs, facilitating financial support for export strategies, monitoring opportunities in international markets and organizing dedicated systemic missions to enter emerging and innovative markets abroad, including the cyber security market.

The Ministry of Foreign Affairs and International Cooperation in cooperation with the Security Intelligence Department and the Ministry of Defence, has organized systemic missions in Washington, London, and many other relevant markets in order to foster the international promotion of national companies specialized in cybersecurity related fields, such as fintech, defence, energy and ICT.

In 2017 was published Italian Cybersecurity Action Plan which sets out the operational guidelines and the actions to be executed in order to implement the National Strategic Framework for Cyberspace Security, as approved by the Italian Prime Minister in his capacity as the political authority responsible for national cybersecurity. The 2017 Action Plan builds on the experience gained in 2014-2015 under the previous Italian Cybersecurity Action Plan (2013) and its review, which led to the adoption on February 17th 2017 of a new Prime Minister Decree currently regulating the Italian cybersecurity architecture. The Plan is also in agreement with the principles behind the reviewing process of Prime Minister Decree January 24th 2013[60]. The process led to the mended National cybersecurity framework as regulated by Prime Minister Decree February 17th 2017. The above mentioned review, jointly conducted by the Administrations that are part of the National cybersecurity framework, greatly benefited from both the lessons learned from the first steps undertaken to build a national cybersecurity system and the experiences and choices adopted by relevant partners and Allies. The outcome of such exercise allowed to identify the changes needed to overcome some difficulties of the past and to envisage a system intended to make it easier for public and private stakeholders to contribute to the implementation of the new Action Plan.

On the 3rd of August 2022 in Italy has been approved the law number 123/2022 on cyber security, that took effect on the 4th of September 2022. This is law is national transformation of the European law 2019/881[61] that was described in the previous chapter on the European framework. This new update of the cyber act add the European standards for the certification of products, service and informatic process, also known as ICT (Information and telecommunication technology). This law give the authority to give this attestation the National Agency for Cybersecurity.

In 2023, regarding the possible change in cybersecurity, Italian government is waiting many possible changes and challenges. Starting for sure with the implantation national wide of the 5G operator and cloud operator that will have to upgrade their system with the National Border of Cybersecurity (Perimetro di Sicurezza Nazionale Cibernetico - PSNC). This new system that is still a work in progress for the EU is putting at the centre of cyber security the National protection of Data. Affected by this new law will be two main actor:

- All subjects that have the head office in Italy and that have an essential role for the government, such as roles that maintain civilian, social o economics activities fundamental for the government
- All subjects that exercise their activities based on web service, IT systems or the one that have poor use of their

protect in which could endanger the national security Within 4 months of the publication of the law this subjects must be identify. In the meantime will be made and published a list of all web and IT system that needs to be updated. But to highlight the main change is the new responsibility given to the new actors identified.

On the 17$^{th}$ of May 2022 by the Italian Prime minister was approved and introduce a new document called the strategy for National Cybersecurity 2022-2026 and the connected plan for the implantation of the strategy. The strategy defined by the ACN (National Cybersecurity Agency), is going to try to implement 82 new measure by the end of 2026, with the main object of:

- Protect strategic national assets by doing a risk based assessment and an efficient framework based on a digital transition
- Respond to threats and crisis of national cybersecurity by monitoring, intercepting, analysing and security process
- Develops digital technology with research activities, excellent centres and specialized industries.

These challenges are designated for the public administrations and private sectors and try to mitigate the constant evolution of cybersecurity threats, trying to stop fake news and trying to guarantee the basic human rights if freedom.

# 2.5 CYBERSECURITY REGULATIONS IN ITALY

In Italy are active at the moment different framework to regulate cybersecurity and in this paragraph they are going to be describe. The latest update that has been approved by the Italian parliament is coming from august 2021 with the law decree n.82[62] that give disposition on urgent manners in the field of cyber security, by defining the architecture of cybersecurity at national level and by making the agency for the national cyber security. The law has been modified and integrated into law by the prime minister of that time President Mario Draghi and giving the role of director of the agency for national cybersecurity to Professor Roberto Baladoni.

The first 4[63] articles of the law-decree defines governance in the national cybersecurity system by placing at the head the prime minister to whom is given the main direction and responsibility of the cybersecurity policy, to whom as well is given the authority to adopt the best national strategy and nominating the heads of the agency for the national cybersecurity. The prime minister can delegate to the authority in charge the information system for the security of the Republic. Is also made the by the prime minister the inter-ministerial committee for cybersecurity (CIC), which duty is to advise, innovate and vigilance policies of cybersecurity.

In detail, article 1[64] gives definitions of main principle used in the decree. Such as the definition of cybersecurity, all necessary activities to protect cyber threats, cyber systems, cyber services and cyber communication, making sure they are available, confidential and untouched, guarantee the resilience of the cyber system in the national cyber space. Very important was the definition that was given to "National cyber space resilience" that refer to activities directed to prevent a prejudgment of national cybersecurity, such a damage to independency, integrity or security of the Republic and democratic institutions, such as those institutions that take interest in politics, army, economics, science and industry in Italy, that could be compromised because of an interruption of the functions essential for the state.

In the article 2[65] the Prime minister is the authority at the head of the architecture of cybersecurity, also:

- Choose the strategy of cybersecurity policy, after discussion with the CIC that is given the definition in the article 4,
- Is going to nominee the director of the new Agency for the national cybersecurity.

In the article 3[66] instead the prime minister can delegate some responsibility to the Authority for the cybersecurity system of the Republic. This Authority must constantly inform the Prime Minister on the activities delegated by the Minister to the authority.

Lastly the article 4[67] complete the governance of the new architecture of the national cyber security and the Agency for the national cyber security, by creating the CIC (inter-ministerial committee for cybersecurity).

Instead the article 5[68] is the one responsible for the institution of the Agency fir the national cybersecurity.

The cyber defence in Italy is integrated in more wide prospect of cybersecurity. After the push of the EU in Italy by a decree of the Prime Minister of that time, Mario Monti, on January 2013 is introduce the very first infrastructure of national cybersecurity. This decree create the first department of information for cybersecurity (DIS), that is the authority responsible for the protection of the cybersecurity in Italy. Also this decree create the NSC (agency for the cybersecurity), that is going to help to an operational level in case of cybersecurity crisis, objective is to prevent and to handle this type of crisis. The last thing that was created in this decree was the CISR (inter-ministerial committee for the cybersecurity of the Republic) of which the duty is to propose to the Prime Minister the strategies to improve national cybersecurity.

Update to the package of law published back in 2013 arrived at the very begging of 2017 with the decree sign by Prime Minister Paolo Gentiloni, this decree is coming by build necessity to have a better structure architecture of cybersecurity to protect industries in national territory. With this decree DIS gets more duties and became the active member of the cybersecurity infrastructure, so the one who makes decision and gives guidelines on the action plan to follow in case of a crisis. Another big change in this decree is the creation of a new validation and certification centre for the implementation of security standard for cyber product that will get to critical infrastructure of the country. All of this changes brought to the creation of a national security net in 2019.

Last update to record is coming from the decree 82 of 2021. This decree change many aspects of the previous legislation in particular the institution of ACN (Agency for the national cybersecurity). The decree is giving financial independency to the agency and jurisdiction independency. The main task of the agency is to make an annual recap on everything that regard national cybersecurity. Also this decree is shifting the responsibility of national cybersecurity from DIS to ACN, but they still work closely to aim the maximum level of cybersecurity. Main task are to schedule and plan the answer in case of cyber threat, and also to plan and act national and international mock up. This agency will receive notification of violation or attempt to violate security of cyber infrastructures. Now the CAN is the leading actor in the national cybersecurity net, with duties to draft the best cybersecurity strategy and achieve safe common actions to reach the maximum national resilience.

National security sensitive information is not just a government business. Private entities operating in strategic sectors must be considered as key assets and included into a holistic approach to national cybersecurity that provides for the implementation of minimum security requirements for Country-critical systems. On these premises, the core tasks were selected for their systemic relevance due to the fact that they:

- Leverage the competences and responsibilities of all relevant stakeholders (public sector, private sector, research and academia).
- Refer to the most relevant activities aimed at consolidating the national cyber defence system including: assets' common protection (CERT); SW/HW certification; identification of critical functions; info-sharing requirements in case of relevant cyber events; etc.

Italian cybersecurity framework has been revised and optimized through:

- The simplification of both ordinary and emergency management procedures
- The reorganization of the National cybersecurity framework
- The simplification of the decision making for cyber crises', aimed at
- facilitating prompt and efficient response and remediation.

Of particular relevance are the measures intended to:

- Assign to the Director General of the Security Intelligence Department a central role among the entities composing

the National cybersecurity Suppress the cyber NISP and relocate the National Cybersecurity Management Board within the Security Intelligence Department. The board will be responsible for cybersecurity crises' management and will be supervised by a Security Intelligence Department Deputy Director.
- Promote close interaction between the National CERT and the Public Administration CERT in order to facilitate their operational coordination and guarantee a single detection capacity, alert, and first cyber incidents' assessment.
- Establish a national evaluation and certification centre, within the Ministry of Economic Development, responsible for security and reliability check of ICT components for Critical Infrastructures.
- Enlarge and better define the number of actors operating in security relevant sectors (Operators of Essential Services and Digital Service Providers) required to notify serious cyber incidents or else to pay effective, proportionate, and dissuasive penalties.

A real improvement of the Italian cybersecurity landscape cannot be achieved without full commitment of public and private stakeholders. For this reason, the Plan aims at engaging relevant private companies, academia and research centres. In particular by involving small and medium business in this system that so far are kept out of the equation as after a risk assessment are not considered as essential to deal with like it would really be.

# 3.1 LATEST CYBER ATTACKS

There are no two ways about it[69]: 2022 was a tough year in all things cybersecurity. With most concerns about remote and hybrid work relatively unchanged from the previous year, 2022 initially seemed like it would follow established trends, with new developments emerging gradually as time went on. Hindsight is always 20/20, though, and 2022 rapidly became another banner year for cybersecurity concerns. Critical infrastructure remained a theme in 2022, as major attacks on vital services like healthcare rose sharply and high-profile incidents made headlines everywhere. Elsewhere, the demand for talented security professionals rose sharply, and issues from years past remained frustratingly persistent. The Russia-Ukraine[70] conflict's cybersecurity implications. Unfortunately, 2022 began with major changes that had wide-reaching implications in the form of the Russia-Ukraine conflict. After nearly two months of tension, Russian troops amassed on the Ukrainian border invaded, leading to a widespread and prolonged conflict. The invasion was preceded by coordinated cyberattacks on 70 Ukrainian government websites, compromising 10 and defacing them with threatening messages; further activity targeting Ukrainian systems involved a wiper ware campaign in February 2022. Russian cyber activity remains largely focused on Ukraine; however, the ongoing conflict presents an increased cybersecurity risk and concern for many organizations worldwide.

In April of 2022[71], Costa Rica experienced two crippling

cyberattacks courtesy of the Conti ransomware gang. These attacks targeted essential services in the country, impacting everything from medical appointment systems to scheduled tax payments, leading to the exposure of an alleged 850 gigabytes of governmental data on top of lost millions. The Costa Rican government declared a state of emergency in response to these ransomware attacks, the first time a government has taken such an action in response to a cybersecurity incident.

Globally, the cybersecurity workforce grew by 11.1% year over year, and yet demand for skilled security professionals continues to outpace the supply of talent. The reasons for this are frustratingly mundane: it takes time and resources to build cybersecurity expertise, both of which are hard to come by for many organizations facing the rising tide of cyberattacks.

The Federal Bureau of Investigation reported that 25%[72] of ransomware attacks in 2022 targeted the healthcare sector. Cybersecurity concerns have been nearly as urgent as the COVID-19 pandemic response for healthcare providers as attackers continued to take advantage of the distractions and uncertainty around continued COVID-19 management. The majority of major healthcare breaches in 2022 were the result of compromised third-party vendors, however, leading to greater scrutiny over organizations' digital supply chains. By no means exclusive to the sector, cybersecurity in the digital supply chain is a theme that began to draw greater attention throughout the year that was.

More tools don't necessarily result in a better security response. In fact, companies with a more complex tech stack often have a harder time detecting and responding to an attack. That's because complex toolsets create noise that becomes easier to tune out over time, leading to what's known as alert fatigue. Imagine dealing with hundreds of alerts from multiple security tools at any given time and sifting through reams of data to try and figure out what's a genuine threat and what's a false positive. To give you a sense of how much cybersecurity approaches have changed over the years, let's take a quick look at some of the solutions that IT has turned to and the approximate year they were introduced[73].

- 1990: Antivirus (AV): Traditional antivirus software is designed to prevent attackers from compromising endpoints and servers, looking for attributes of known malicious files. In the mid-2010s, "next-generation antivirus" became a popular term used to market additional AV functionality. Used in isolation or as the core tool in a set, these programs can lack the comprehensive functionality needed to address all the threats facing a business.

- 2005: Security Information and Event Management (SIEM) software: SIEM software aggregates data and logs from tools like firewalls, antivirus software, and other detection sources. SIEM software can be costly, not to mention complex to set up and manage, as it requires careful configuration and testing to establish rules for detection. False positives are common in these cases.

- 2013: Endpoint Detection and Response (EDR): EDR deploys an agent on an endpoint to collect data types beyond logs, enabling continuous monitoring on the endpoint—but data still needs to be analysed by a mature security team or dedicated managed security service provider (MSSP), and the sheer volume of it can easily lead to alert fatigue when automation or support is not available.

- 2016: Security Orchestration, Automation, and Response (SOAR) solutions: SOAR solutions aggregate information from other programs that are often not designed to work together in the first place. SOAR aims to simplify security tool management and solve the problem of tech stack complexity but can lack the cohesion and ease of use of a holistic solution.

- 2016 to now: Managed Detection and Response (MDR):

Managed Detection and Response takes the benefits of EDR's continuous monitoring a step further, delivering its benefits as a managed service. This allows companies of any size to get security expertise on their side.

Adding new technology to manage security has quickly become an outdated approach. Each new tool is another budget line item, and growing toolsets demand even more time to oversee. Each tool may only provide a view into one aspect of your IT environment, resulting in a siloed approach to threat management. What's more, integrating new tools is another time-consuming task; finding interoperable tools that scale to your security needs is tough. The shift to remote work has only made this more apparent, with additional challenges from the use of shadow IT solutions, tools and software that an IT team doesn't have total control or knowledge of, that staff may put in place to support their new work setup.

In the last couple of years in Europe, especially since the begging of the war between Ukraine and Russia, we saw an exponential growth of cyberattacks. Following is going to be listed the most famous attacks[74]:

-   In August 2022, the Finnish parliament's website experienced a DDoS attack while the parliament was in session. This denial-of-service attack may be part of a coordinated campaign by Russian state-sponsored hackers to disrupt the Finnish government's websites in retaliation for the application to join NATO. A DDoS attack temporarily blocks access to a website but does not cause permanent destruction.
-   The Russian "hacktivist" group called the People's Cyber Army engaged 7.25 million bots in August 2022 in a bot attack to take the Energoatom website down. It used a flood of garbage web traffic and webpage requests. A disruption of online services lasted for a few hours, but no permanent negative impact remained. The attack was part of a Russian psyops campaign to create fear of a nuclear

disaster and terrorize Europeans.

- Greek national gas distributor DESFA reported an incidence of a cyber-attack in August 2022. The attack impacted part of the company's IT infrastructure and caused a data leak. The ransomware operation of cybercriminals called Ragnar Locker is holding the stolen data hostage. They demand ransom not to expose sensitive data. The company refused to make a payment.

- In August 2022, the South Staffordshire Water Company reported an attack that caused a network disruption in its internal corporate network and a data loss. A cybercriminal ransomware group threatened to tamper with the water supplied by the company. The company disputed this claim. The criminals demanded payment to not release sensitive files and explain how the network breach happened.

- The government of Montenegro's digital IT infrastructure reported an unprecedented cyberattack in August 2022. No data breach occurred. However, certain governmental services and telecommunications experienced disruption, including border crossings and airport operations. The state-owned utility company, EPCG, switched to manual operations as a precautionary measure.

- A DDoS attack disrupted many Estonian government websites for several hours in April 2022. The attack targeted websites for the president, the Ministry of Foreign Affairs, the Police and Border Guard, the identification card webpage, and the state services digital portal. Estonia's condemnation of the Russian war on Ukraine makes the country a target for Russian hackers.

- The Iranian Islamic Culture and Communication Organization (ICCO) experienced a severe attack in July 2022. Six ICCO websites went down, and 15 others changed to photos of Massoud Rajaivi, the Iranian Resistance leader. Additionally, there was data destruction on 44 servers and hundreds of computers. The ICCO also lost 35 databases with highly-confidential information about money laundering, spies, and terrorists living abroad.

- In July 2022, the Belgian government announced that three Chinese hacker groups, part of the known Chinese Advanced Persistent Threat actors, attacked Belgian public services and military defence forces. The Chinese government-sponsored attackers steal trade secrets and intelligence information. The Soft Cell Chinese group recently launched a new remote access trojan (RAT) malware in June 2022.

- Hackers took over the Twitter account of the British Army in July 2022. The social media account underwent multiple name and photo changes. The content started promoting contests to win Angry Apes non-fungible tokens (NFTs), digital art stored on a blockchain. The army's YouTube page experienced an attack as well. Its name changed to Ark Invest, and the account promoted interviews of Elon Musk talking about cryptocurrency.

- A DDoS attack in July 2022 blocked access to the website of the Lithuanian energy company, Ignitis Group. The company managed the attack and limited the damage using DDoS Protection. No data breach occurred, but the attacks were persistent and ongoing. Pro-Russia group Killnet claimed responsibility. The attack retaliated against Lithuanian support of Ukraine in the war with Russia.

As this major attack were happening all around Europe also in the rest of the world many attacks were taking place, such us[75]:

- One of the most damaging recent cyberattacks was a Microsoft Exchange server compromise that resulted in several zero-day vulnerabilities. The vulnerabilities, known as ProxyLogon and initially launched by the Hafnium hacking group, were first spotted by Microsoft in January and patched in March. However, more groups joined Hafnium in attacking unpatched systems, resulting in thousands of organizations being compromised.

- Dating app MeetMindful suffered a cybersecurity attack in January 2021, resulting in data of more than 2 million users being stolen and leaked. The hacking group behind the event managed to steal information like users' full names and Facebook account tokens.

- In March 2021, cyber criminals threatened to leak documents from the Tether cryptocurrency. The attackers claimed the data would "harm the Bitcoin ecosystem" and demanded a settlement fee of around 500 Bitcoin ($24 million), but Tether refused to pay.

- A ransomware attack on insurance firm CNA Financial left employees locked out of their systems and blocked from accessing corporate resources. The attack in March 2021 also involved company data being stolen, which led CNA Financial to reportedly pay the $40 million settlement fee.

- Data of more than 530 million Facebook users, including their names, Facebook IDs, dates of birth, and relationship status, was published online in April 2021. Facebook, now Meta, said the information was obtained through scraping in 2019.

- The growing threat that advanced cybersecurity attacks pose to the world was highlighted by the Colonial Pipeline attack in May 2021. The fuel pipeline operator suffered a ransomware attack launched by the DarkSide hacking group, which led to fuel disruption and mass panic buying across the U.S.

- An unauthorized entry cyberattack in May 2021 resulted in the exposure of 1.7 million users of the Japanese dating app Omiai.

- In June 2021, Audi and Volkswagen revealed a data breach had affected more than 3.3 million customers and prospective buyers, who were primarily U.S.-based. The breach was blamed on an associated vendor, which was purportedly responsible for exposing the data between

August 2019 and May 2021.

- The United Kingdom's trading website for guns and shooting equipment revealed that records of 100,000 gun owners had been stolen and published online in July 2021. Gun ownership is strictly controlled in the U.K., so the data breach of customers' names and addresses caused significant privacy and safety concerns.

- In August 2021, telecoms firm T-Mobile suffered a cybersecurity breach that led to the data of around 50 million existing customers and prospects being stolen. The data, which included customer addresses, drivers' licenses, and social security numbers, was stolen by a 21-year-old, who claimed to have obtained around 106GB of information.

- An attack on Poly Network in August 2021 proved that cybersecurity breaches on cryptocurrency firms are on the rise. The blockchain firm revealed an Ethereum smart contract hack resulted in cyber criminals stealing cryptocurrency worth more than $600 million.

- Cybersecurity attacks on medical organizations and healthcare firms are also increasing. As a result of the hack on AP-HP, a Paris public hospital system, in September 2021, cyber criminals stole personal data belonging to around 1.4 million people who were tested for COVID-19 in 2020.

- Cream Finance, a decentralized finance firm, suffered a vulnerability in its project's market system. The hack, which was revealed in September 2021, caused losses worth $34 million.

- A South African debt recovery company suffered a significant attack that led to client and employee data being illegally accessed from its servers in September 2021. The incident is suspected to have affected the personally identifiable information (PII), including owed debts, of over 1.4 million people.

- Department store Neiman Marcus suffered a data breach

that resulted in the exposure and theft of up to 3.1 million customers' payment card details. The attack was detected in September 2021 but began in May 2020, and most of the data stolen was believed to have been from expired or invalid cards.

- A hacker, who claimed to have leaked the entire database of Argentina's National Registry of Persons, has allegedly stolen the data of more than 45 million Argentinian residents. However, the government denied the hack.

- The value of a cryptocurrency linked to but not officially associated with the Netflix program Squid Game plummeted after a suspected exit scam in November 2021. The cryptocurrency's value dropped from $2,850 to $0.003028 overnight, which resulted in investors losing millions of dollars.

- Also in November 2021, a data breach of the trading app Robinhood affected the data of around 5 million users. Data like usernames, email addresses, and phone numbers were compromised through a customer support system.

- Yet another cybersecurity attack against digital currencies, BitMart suffered a breach that enabled cyber criminals to steal approximately $150 million worth of cryptocurrency in December 2021. The attack resulted in total losses of around $200 million, including damages.

- In December 2021, a zero-day vulnerability was discovered in the Log4j Java library. The remote code execution flaw is now active, and the resulting bug, Log4Shell, is being activated by botnets like Mirai.

- HR platform Kronos suffered a ransomware attack that took the Kronos Private Cloud offline. The outage occurred shortly before Christmas and took the vital service down for several weeks.

- In August 2020, credit reporting agency Experian suffered a breach that affected 24 million consumers in South Africa and more than 793,000 businesses. The incident occurred when an individual who claimed to be a client requested services that prompted the data's release. The stolen data was eventually secured and deleted, while Experian revealed it had not been used fraudulently and that its customer database, infrastructure, and systems had not been compromised.

- The data of more than 10.6 million customers of MGM Resorts hotels was leaked to a hacking forum in February 2020. The data included addresses, dates of birth, email addresses, names, and phone numbers belonging to celebrities, business executives, government employees, and tourists. However, the hack did not breach users' credit card details. The incident began in mid-2019 when MGM discovered unauthorized access to its server. Another data breach followed in February 2020, which saw user data published on an open, accessible forum.

- The University of California, based in San Francisco, suffered a ransomware attack that led to hackers demanding a settlement payment of $3 million on June 1, 2020. The university's system was targeted by malware that could encrypt various servers and steal and encrypt critical data. The university negotiated and paid a settlement fee of $1.14 million but later revealed no data had been compromised.

- Technology and consulting firm Cognizant was affected by the Maze ransomware attack on April 18, 2020. The attackers stole data and threatened to publish it online unless Cognizant paid a settlement fee. Cognizant later revealed it paid a ransom fee of between $50 million and $70 million to restore its services.

- Tillamook County's IT systems were infected by encryption malware on January 22, 2020. The attack shut down its computer and phone systems and took down the website that hosts its various departments. Tillamook County's computer systems were down for at least two weeks, and attackers demanded $300,000 as settlement, which would double after two weeks, to restore the data.

The county tried to avoid paying the settlement fee but could not restore the data and eventually settled.

- As the COVID-19 pandemic broke, an attack targeting the World Health Organization (WHO) resulted in the breach of 25,000 email addresses and passwords. The data was leaked online on April 19, 2020, along with information belonging to other groups fighting the pandemic, including the Gates Foundation, the National Institutes of Health (NIH), and the U.S. Centers for Disease Control and Prevention (CDC).

- Videoconferencing service Zoom saw a massive increase in activity throughout 2020 with people working from home and speaking to friends and family through the application. However, in April 2020, a cyberattack known as Zoombombing enabled cyber criminals to join private meetings, access conversations, and share offensive images, videos, and screens. Zoom updated its application to enhance security levels.

- A Mitsubishi Electric systems data breach resulted in around 200 MB of files being stolen. The breach, which was first detected in June 2019 but was reported in January 2020, contained employee and applicant information, data about retired employees from affiliate companies, and sales and technical material. The attack was caused by a vulnerability in the organization's antivirus solution, which Chinese hackers exploited.

- One of the most significant cyber-attacks that occurred in 2020 was through a hacker known as ShinyHunters. The hacker stole around 386 million user records from 18 different companies between the start of the year and July. The attacker posted links to these companies' databases, made them freely available to download, and sold data online.

As all of this was happening all around the world also Italy was being target by the so called "NoName"[76], a Russian group of hackers that was targeting all nations who were helping Ukraine during the conflict. 22$^{nd}$ of February 2023, the brown bear, symbol of Russia, is dancing, with a big smile and nice suite, next to the Italian flag. This is how the NoName group signed the cyberattack against Italian cybersecurity system. An attack discover on the early morning of the 22$^{nd}$ of February that attack one after the other many institutional website: 4 ministries (defence ministry, foreign ministry, agriculture polices ministry and the main ministry for the publication of national identification card), Carabinieri, TIM, Bper bank and A2A energy. The result of this attacks were visible few minutes after the begging of the attack: access to the web site limited until got completely blocked, with all representative scheme substitute by pop-up windows for maintenance or web site inaccessible. To take the ownership of this attack, two days after the official visit of the Italian prime minister Giorgia Meloni in Kiev, in which the Italian prime minister met the Ukrainian prime minister Volodymyr Zelensky, were the NoName57 hacker group, born in March 2022, few weeks after the begging of Russian invasions, and call in this new group all expert that mainly use as weapon of attack the ddos (Distributed denial of service). The DDOS is a system in which thousands of infected computers send from everywhere around the world an enormous quantity of data against a selected target with the goal of paralyzing the activities. So all systems become full and incapable of working. On the telegram channels, this collective that count 28 thousands subscriber, started to make fun of this attack by making fun with the cheapest irony against Italy, with the image of a bear that is dancing on some fusilli, an Italian type of pasta, with the words "mamma mia", but not only irony also a clear statement to explain the reasons behind the attack that was stating: "After breakfast with the French croissant we went to eat Italian pizza, who which will provide to Ukraine the sixth package of military assistance, that includes 3 types of air defence systems. Giorgia Melone duting the press conference in

Kiev stated that those systems will be Sampt-t, Skyguard and Spike. We will keep traveling inside the Russia phobic Italy ". Italy was attack straight after France, that was hit with a very similar attack during the night between the 21$^{st}$ and 22$^{nd}$ of February. For many hours the attack was successful until the defence system against the ddos start to work and the cyber police intervene and mitigate the attack by bringing the system back almost to normality.

Even if the attack was controlled that alert state remain at maximum level as underlined by the national cyber security agency that stated: "most of the services were promptly brought back to normality: an alarm was launch and the defence system react very well. The attack was directed to multiple applications that target public and private industry." Threats are behind every corner as stated by red hot cyber, a web site which focus is cyberattacks, for example in the dark web an hacker was trying to sell access to carabinieri web site that is a very important military web site full of critical data, the access that the hacker was trying to sell were of very important persons in the system with many access to government systems.

This type of attack is typical way of attacking institutional and private website. Luckly is a show off attack instead of disruptive attack, it is more to send a strong political message. The final objective of this type of attack is not to steal data or to block completely systems like the latest ransomware attacks. In fact who claim this attack is the Noname57, which communicates through the telegram channel with 28000 subscriber, a group that like it was said before, born in March 2022, few weeks after the Russian invasion and recognise itself as a protector of freedom in alliance with Russia. Many of the attacks claimed by this group were targeting Ukraine, USA and European countries.

This particular offence started on the 21$^{st}$ of February, on the same day the Italian prime minister was visiting Ukraine. The first web site that was attack was in fact not casually the ministry of defence web site, clear signal against the 6$^{th}$ help package that Italy was sending to Ukraine in response to Russian invasion. So the NoName started a ddos attack, in particular that was an attack that enter in the category of the ddos attack but a little bit different. This particular attack is called "Slow Http Attack". The hacker send an Http request with a very low speed, Http stands for HyperTextTransfer Protocol, is a protocol that constitutes a lintel of the web. An Http is built with an alphanumerical string that always end with 2 characters in "newline (\n\n). It is a signal that is intended to say my command end here. By slowing a lot this request, the hacker put the server in a position to wait for the  newline code for ever. In this way the server needs to keep up a lot of connection in the same time, until the system collapse. Users that try to connect will not manage to complete the task. This type of attacks are very easy to put in place as the hacker doesn`t need many machine at the same time but it could be done also with very few asset, even with only one computer.

# 3.2 NEW ENVIRONMENT OF WORKING AND CONSEQUENTIAL THREATS

Security and IT teams everywhere are feeling the burn from the year that was 2022. There are new threats, too many tools and alerts, far too much for IT to manage. Cyber threats are constantly evolving as attackers uncover new exploits which means that you need an effective solution that can always stay a step ahead. Not all companies can afford a CISO, let alone an in-house team of cybersecurity professionals, which only compounds these issues; the need trained staff to manage security systems, after all. This year, a new approach to cybersecurity is needed. This new approach starts with a holistic solution that empowers companies with a continuous view into network, endpoints, and the cloud, allowing to identify, prioritize, triage, and respond to cyber threats. Coupled with ongoing training and education for staff, companies will build strong security habits to better defend against potential attacks.

The company springs into action to minimize potential damages to customers, employees, shareholders and others. A quick, effective response helps avoid negative publicity, lawsuits and regulatory inquiries. Already this scenario is bad enough, but now imagine a company operations or environmental manager and arrive that day when they find that an on-going pipeline release had been occurring undetected over the weekend because someone hacked the computer system and disabled a leak detection alarms. The Internet-based systems could have detected and quickly stopped this release, but now it is an environmental catastrophe. Over the next few days after the attack the company realize the far-reaching consequences of an unsecure computer server include emergency response and environmental remediation expenses, regulatory agency fines and penalties, third party bodily injury and property damage claims, and a public relations nightmare. Business interruption is projected to be significant because forensic cyber specialists must be hired to review the computer systems to help restore operations. The future of the company in the balance.

Most people associate cyber incidents with identity theft, loss of assets/money, and theft of company proprietary data, patents, and sensitive information. However, today the business world and technologies advance so rapidly that threats continue to change and expand seemingly daily. Computer system hacking, denial of service attacks, malware, ransomware, data selling, identity theft, and trading of sensitive information incidents continue to make headlines. These crimes can even extend to corporate spying, state espionage, cyberterrorism, and cyber warfare. This increased public awareness, along with government and regulatory cyber initiatives, should leave little doubt that many critical industries have existing and emerging risks and exposures. Cyber security along with physical security is vital to critical industries such as: energy, transportation, telecommunications, financial services, energy production and transmission, public services/utilities, and chemical and manufacturing industries, as it was discussed in the previous paragraphs. Most businesses have some vulnerability to a cyber incident, but particularly if they rely on complex supervisory control and data acquisition (SCADA) systems.

Let's now analysed the new environment of working and the various types of cyber intrusions and attacks and how they can pose a significant pollution liability risk. Cyber-crime can result in loss of control of critical equipment and warning systems and has the potential to cause damage to human health and the environment from catastrophic spills, waste discharges, and air emissions. These events can cause fires, explosions and hazardous material releases that result in bodily injury, property damage, environmental remediation expense, and significant legal liability claims.

Terms such as cyber-crime and cyber terrorism seem to be interchangeable and somewhat confusing. Cyber-crime is generally defined as a crime in which a computer is the target or is used as a tool to commit an offense. Generally, cyber-crimes fall into one of three categories depending on whether they involve, people, property, or the government. One of the most common cyber-crimes in the news these days are ransomware attacks, particularly on municipalities, where the criminal installs a virus that encrypts files or otherwise damages computer systems. To restore the system, the criminal requires an electronic payment by a deadline and often increases the ransom if the deadline is not met. Broadly, cyber terrorism uses the internet to conduct violent acts that result in, or threaten, loss of life or significant bodily harm, in order to achieve political or ideological gains through threat or intimidation. Cyber terrorist activities can include deliberate, large-scale disruption of computer networks, especially of personal computers connected to the Internet, using tools such as computer viruses or worms, phishing e-mails, or insertion of malicious programming scripts, software or hardware. Differentiating between cyber-crime and cyber terrorism can be difficult, but both types of incidents can have devastating effects. Consider a cyber-crime involving a ransomware attack on an industrial facility, but with the hacker also having the ability to use the same computer system to retaliate for a late ransom payment. Retaliation could include something as dramatic as causing a release of hazardous chemicals that threatens loss of life or causes pollution of the surrounding environment. This is a clearly a cyber-crime, but if done in conjunction with a political ideology or to illicit a social response, it may be defined as cyber terrorism.

As the "Internet of Things" continues to expand, cyber security continues to grow more critical. Vulnerabilities highlight the need for environmental and operations staff to work together in identifying worst case scenarios and the operational systems that are most vital in preventing a pollution event. Only then can they work with IT security professionals to address the exposures. The following are some examples of key vulnerabilities and systems associated with several critical industries (Cooperative Cybersecurity Capabilities (RC3) Program; National Rural Electric Cooperative[77]:

-   Pipelines can be very vulnerable to cyber-attack based on their extensive use of SCADA systems to remotely operate the pipeline, control inputs and outputs, and perform critical leak detection. Threats to SCADA may come not only in the form of physical terrorism, but from general Internet threats, (phishing, hackers), errors resulting from ineffective training programs, or even disgruntled employees.

-   These industries make extensive use of Distributed Control Systems (DCSs) and Programmable Logic Controllers (PLCs) that can be vulnerable to cyber-attack. Control of DCSs and PLCs by an outsider can lead to severe consequences including fire, explosion or environmental release. Care must be taken to prevent access to both the industrial equipment computer systems as well as to ensure the physical security of the devices and assets being controlled or monitored. Further, increased security measures are needed as plant industrial control systems (ICSs) become more integrated with other potentially vulnerable corporate computer systems.

- A single tanker accident can result in release of millions of gallons of crude oil that causes an environmental disaster and long lasting natural resource damages. Maritime activity has long relied on GPS technology, but is also increasingly relying on ICT to meet the demands of customers and provide transportation safety. ICT is used to deliver and optimize operations that include ship propulsion, navigation, freight management, traffic control, predictive maintenance and communications. The vulnerabilities created by security gaps in ICT systems within the maritime sector can also introduce risk to other commonly shared infrastructure and systems. Ship to shore pipelines and bulk storage systems can also be exposed. Systems used to manage and treat oily bilge water can also be vulnerable.

- An attack on the SCADA system used in water treatment and distribution systems can significantly alter the system's performance and negatively impact public health and safety.

- In addition to marine transportation, air transport has also proven to be vulnerable to cyber security breaches. Airports continue to assess their security needs beyond passenger screening.

In this new environment al type of enterprises must have an adequate response to the current threats, but especially prepare for the future by anticipating future threats. In the world of digitalization, it is important to develop an awareness of internet security tips. Gaining this knowledge and applying it makes you less prone to cyber-attacks. This requires a lot of effort and time. According to Internet Live Stats, more than 145TB of internet traffic takes place each second. As such, the internet has become a digital Silk Road that facilitates nearly every facet of modern life. And just as ancient merchants were sometimes beset by bandits on the actual Silk Road, today's entrepreneurs can easily find themselves under attack from cyber malcontents working to derail companies through theft and disruption. Business owners may not know when an attack could occur, but taking proper precautions can hamper or completely stymie a hacker's attempt to access your network. According to Verizon's 2021 Data Breach Investigations Report, 46% of breaches impacted small and medium size businesses. When it comes to starting a small business, new owners have many decisions to make and often leave cybersecurity measures by the wayside. Unless they focus on shoring up their defences, they may inadvertently end up leaving points of entry wide open for hackers. That can be a major problem. A joint report by IBM and the Ponemon Institute found that the average cost of a data breach increased by 10% in 2021, and Verizon's data indicates that the cost of 95% of incidents for SMBs fell between 826 euros and 653,587 euros. What's more, these businesses often lack the resources to defend themselves successfully from attacks. Stephen Cobb, an independent researcher and consultant who studies technology and risk, said that small businesses fall into hackers' cybersecurity sweet spot, since they "have more digital assets to target than an individual consumer has but less security than a larger enterprise." Couple that with the costs associated with implementing proper defences, and the business have a situation primed for intrusions. Since security breaches can be devastating to small businesses, owners are more likely to pay a ransom to get their data back. SMBs can also merely be a stepping stone for attackers to gain access to larger businesses. Regardless of their target, hackers generally aim to gain access to a company's sensitive data, such as consumers' credit card information. With enough identifying information, attackers can then exploit an individual's identity in any number of damaging ways. One of the best ways to prepare for an attack is to understand the different methods hackers generally use to gain access to that information. While this is by no means an exhaustive list of potential threats, since cybercrime is a constantly evolving phenomenon, companies should at least be aware of the following types of attacks.

- APT: An advanced persistent threat, or APT, is a long-term targeted attack in which a hacker breaks into a network in multiple phases to avoid detection. Once an attacker gains access to the target network, they work to remain undetected while establishing their foothold on the system. If a breach is detected and repaired, the attacker may have already secured other routes into the system so they can continue to plunder data.
- DDoS: A distributed denial-of-service attack occurs when a server is intentionally overloaded with requests until it shuts down the target's website or network system.
- Inside attack: An inside attack occurs when someone with administrative privileges, usually from within the organization, purposely misuses their credentials to gain access to confidential company information. Former employees, in particular, present a threat, particularly if they left the company on bad terms. Business should have a protocol in place to revoke all access to company data immediately when an employee is terminated.
- Malware: This umbrella term is short for "malicious software" and covers any program introduced into the target's computer with the intent to cause damage or gain unauthorized access. Types of malware include viruses, worms, Trojans, ransomware and spyware. Knowing this is important because it helps the company determine the type of cybersecurity software the company needs.
- Man in the middle (MitM) attack: In any normal transaction, two parties exchange goods – or, in the case of e-commerce, digital information – with each other. Knowing this, a hacker who uses the MitM method of intrusion does so by installing malware that interrupts the flow of information to steal important data. This is generally done when one or more parties conduct the transaction through an unsecured public Wi-Fi network,

where the hacker has installed malware that sifts through data.

- Password attack: There are three main types of password attacks: a brute-force attack, which involves guessing at passwords until the hacker gets in; a dictionary attack, which uses a program to try different combinations of dictionary words; and keylogging, which tracks a user's keystrokes, including login IDs and passwords.

- Phishing: Perhaps the most commonly deployed form of cybertheft, phishing attacks involve collecting sensitive information like login credentials and credit card information through a legitimate-looking (but ultimately fraudulent) website that's often sent to unsuspecting individuals in an email. Spear phishing, an advanced form of this type of attack, requires in-depth knowledge of specific individuals and social engineering to gain their trust and infiltrate the network.

- Ransomware: A ransomware attack infects your machine with malware and, as the name suggests, demands a ransom. Typically, ransomware either locks you out of your computer and demands money in exchange for regaining access, or it threatens to publish private information if you don't pay a specified amount. Ransomware is one of the fastest-growing types of security breaches.

- SQL injection attack: For more than four decades, web developers have been using Structured Query Language (SQL) as one of the main coding languages on the internet. While a standardized language has greatly benefited the internet's development, it can also be an easy way for malicious code to make its way onto business's website. Through a successful SQL injection attack on companies servers, bad actors can access and modify important databases, download files and even manipulate devices on the network.

- Zero-day attack: Zero-day attacks can be a developer's

worst nightmare. They are unknown flaws and exploits in software and systems discovered by attackers before the developers and security staff become aware of any threats. These exploits can go undiscovered for months or even years until they're discovered and repaired.

One of the attack that put on its knees cybersecurity happened in 2017, when the declared impossible to hack WPA2 was hacked. Early Monday morning of 16/10/2017 it was announced that WPA2, WiFi's most popular encryption standard, had been cracked. A new attack method called KRACK (for Key Reinstallation Attack) is now able to break WPA2 encryption, allowing a hacker to read information passing between a device and its wireless access point using a variation of a common – and usually highly detectable – man in the middle attack. If successful, this vulnerability can potentially allow a hacker to spy on your data as well as gain access to unsecured devices sharing the same WiFi network. Of course, as computing power grows, it was just a matter of time before another encryption protocol was broken. In this case, Belgian security researchers at KU Leuven university, led by security expert Mathy Vanhoef, discovered the weakness and published details of the flaw on Monday morning. Essentially, KRACK breaks the WPA2 protocol by "forcing nonce reuse in encryption algorithms" used by Wi-Fi. In cryptography, a nonce is an arbitrary number that may only be used once. It is often a random or pseudo-random number issued in the public key component of an authentication protocol to ensure that old communications cannot be reused. As it turns out, the random numbers used on WPA2 aren't quite random enough, allowing the protocol to be broken. The US Computer Emergency Readiness Team (CERT) issued a warning on Sunday in response to the vulnerability that reads in part that, "The impact of exploiting these vulnerabilities includes decryption, packet replay, TCP connection hijacking, HTTP content injection and others." Even if it is possible an attacker needs to be in reasonably close proximity in order to capture the traffic between an endpoint device and the vulnerable wireless access point. In addition, the attack is unlikely to affect the security of information sent over a connection using additional encrypted methods such as SSL. Every time someone access an HTTPS site the browser creates a separate layer of encryption that will keep the connection safe when doing things like online banking or making purchases, even in spite of this latest security threat. Likewise, VPN connections will continue to protect business corporate data even if your WPA2 connection is compromised.

As more companies grow their businesses online, the need for robust cybersecurity measures grows in lockstep. According to Cybersecurity Ventures' 2022 Cybersecurity Almanac, worldwide spending on such products will increase to a cumulative 1.75 trillion euros for the period 2021 to 2025, up from 1 trillion euros cumulatively for 2017 to 2021. Small businesses looking to ensure their networks have at least a fighting chance against many attacks should be open to installing basic security software.

Cybersecurity has become a critical issue for businesses and individuals alike, as the threat of cyber-attacks continues to grow. The increasing amount of sensitive information being stored and transmitted online has made it more important than ever to protect against cybercrime. Despite the fact that cybersecurity measures have improved significantly in recent years, so too have the techniques of cyber criminals. As a result, the future of cybersecurity looks set to be a constant battle between those who would protect information and those who would steal it. One of the biggest trends in the future of cybersecurity is the use of artificial intelligence (AI) and machine learning (ML) technologies. AI and ML algorithms are able to analyse large amounts of data and detect patterns and anomalies that may indicate a potential threat. This allows organizations to quickly identify and respond to cyber-attacks, reducing the risk of damage and minimizing the impact of a breach. AI-powered cybersecurity solutions can also be used to automate repetitive security tasks, freeing up human resources to focus on more complex issues. AI and ML can also be used to predict future cyber threats, based on historical data and trends. This will allow organizations to proactively defend against potential threats, reducing the risk of successful attacks. Another trend in the future of cybersecurity is the use of blockchain technology. Blockchain is a decentralized ledger that can be used to securely store and transfer information. Because of its decentralized nature, it is much harder for cyber criminals to compromise a blockchain network, and so it is becoming increasingly popular for applications that require high levels of security. This is particularly true for industries such as finance, healthcare, and government, where the risk of data breaches can have serious consequences. The rise of the Internet of Things (IoT) is also set to have a major impact on the future of cybersecurity. IoT devices are becoming increasingly common, and are often used to control critical systems and infrastructure. However, many IoT devices have poor security features, and can be easily compromised by cyber criminals. As a result, organizations will need to implement better security measures to protect against IoT-related cyber threats. This may include updating the firmware and software on IoT devices, or replacing them with more secure devices with multiple levels of security like 2FA. Another major trend in cybersecurity is the increasing focus on collaboration between organizations. In the past, organizations have often been reluctant to share information about cyber threats, for fear of revealing their own vulnerabilities. However, this is changing, as organizations recognize that cyber threats are often too complex for any single organization to tackle alone. In response, many organizations are forming partnerships and sharing information to help protect against cyber-attacks. This includes sharing threat intelligence, best practices, and resources, as well as participating in joint cyber security operations. Cybersecurity also has a major impact on national security, and governments are taking steps to protect their critical infrastructure from cyber-attacks. One example of this is the increasing use of 'zero trust' security models, where access to sensitive information is strictly controlled and monitored. This approach reduces the risk of unauthorized access and helps to prevent cyber-attacks. Governments are also investing in research and development to stay ahead of the latest cyber threats, and to develop new technologies to better protect against these threats. This may include the development of new encryption algorithms, or the use of quantum computing to crack complex codes. The future of cybersecurity and quantum computing is intertwined, as quantum computing has the potential to revolutionize the way data is protected and processed. Currently, most encryption algorithms used for cybersecurity rely on the fact that certain mathematical problems are difficult to solve with classical computers. However, quantum computers have the ability to solve these problems much more quickly, potentially rendering existing encryption methods obsolete. On one hand, this means that quantum computers could be used to break existing encryption, posing a significant threat to cybersecurity. On the other hand, it also means that quantum computers could be used to develop new and more secure forms of encryption, offering unprecedented levels of protection for sensitive information. One potential use of quantum computing in cybersecurity is the development of quantum algorithms to detect and respond to cyber-attacks. These algorithms could be used to analyse large amounts of data and detect patterns that may indicate a potential threat, allowing organizations to quickly identify and respond to cyber-attacks. Additionally, quantum algorithms could be used to predict future cyber threats, based on historical data and trends. Cybersecurity and cloud computing are closely related, as the increased use of cloud computing has led to new security challenges and concerns. Cloud computing allows organizations to store and process data on remote servers, rather than on local devices, providing many benefits such as increased scalability and cost savings. However, the fact that sensitive data is stored on remote servers makes it more vulnerable to cyber-attacks. One of the biggest security concerns with cloud computing is the risk of unauthorized access to sensitive information. This can occur if cyber criminals are able to compromise the security of the cloud provider's servers, or if they are able to steal login credentials or other information that allows them to access the cloud-stored data. To mitigate this risk, organizations need to implement strong access controls and encryption, and use trusted cloud providers that implement robust security measures. Another security concern with cloud computing is the risk of data breaches. This can occur if cyber criminals are able to penetrate the security of the cloud provider's servers and access sensitive information stored on these servers. To minimize this risk, organizations need to ensure that their data is encrypted both in transit and at rest, and that they are using cloud providers that implement strong security measures to protect against data breaches. In addition to these security concerns, there are also compliance and regulatory considerations that organizations need to be aware of when using cloud computing. For example, organizations that deal with sensitive information such as personal data or financial information, may be subject to strict regulations such as the EU's General Data Protection Regulation (GDPR) or the US' Sarbanes-Oxley Act. These regulations dictate the way that sensitive information can be stored, processed, and transmitted, and organizations need to ensure that they are in compliance with these regulations when using cloud computing. To address these security concerns and regulatory requirements, many cloud providers are offering a range of security features, such as encryption, access controls, and monitoring. Organizations can also implement security measures such as multi-factor authentication, intrusion detection systems, and firewalls, to further enhance the security of their cloud-stored data. The integration of 5G technology into the world of telecommunications presents both opportunities and challenges for cybersecurity. On one hand, 5G technology offers faster and more reliable communication, as well as increased connectivity, which can be beneficial for various industries and applications. On the other hand, 5G technology also introduces new security risks, as the increased speed and connectivity can be used by cyber criminals to launch more sophisticated and damaging attacks. One major concern with 5G technology is the risk of cyber-attacks on 5G networks. 5G networks are designed to support millions of devices, which can make them a prime target for cyber criminals. Additionally, 5G networks use software-defined networking (SDN) which makes them more vulnerable to attacks that can take advantage of software vulnerabilities. To minimize this risk, organizations need to implement strong security measures, such as encryption, access controls, and intrusion detection systems, and they need to ensure that they are using trusted 5G network providers that implement robust security measures. Another security concern with 5G technology is the risk of IoT devices becoming compromised. IoT devices are expected to play a significant role in the 5G ecosystem, and these devices often have limited computing power and security features, making them vulnerable to attacks. To minimize this risk, organizations need to ensure that their IoT devices are properly secured, and that they are using trusted IoT device manufacturers that implement strong security measures. Furthermore, 5G technology also introduces new privacy concerns. 5G networks are designed to support a wide range of applications and services, which can result in large amounts of sensitive information being transmitted over the network. To minimize this risk, organizations need to ensure that their sensitive information is encrypted both in transit and at rest, and they need to ensure that they are using trusted 5G network providers that implement strong privacy measures. In addition to technology and collaboration, the future of cybersecurity will also be shaped by regulation and legal frameworks. Governments are increasingly passing laws and regulations aimed at protecting sensitive information, and holding organizations accountable for data breaches. This includes laws that require organizations to implement certain security measures, such as encryption and multi-factor authentication, as well as laws that set penalties for data breaches. Organizations will need to stay informed about the latest laws and regulations.

# 3.3 WHAT IS IN THE NEAR FUTURE OF CYBER SECURITY

Cybersecurity exposures for all businesses will continue to evolve and increase over time. Some of the emerging risks that are likely to become more prominent include[78]:

- New 5G digital networks have already been installed in some areas and are anticipated to be built out in additional market areas in ways that will transform the world. Standards and processes for acceptable 5G system cybersecurity are still being established. Risks will continue to emerge from the unintended introduction of network vulnerabilities in development of new software applications and updates. These larger networks will also be more at risk since more devices will be connected under 5G and the impacts could be more widespread. Also, there is a risk of legacy vulnerabilities in 4G LTE networks that will initially be integrated with 5G networks.
- The cloud services required a data security management whether in transmission or at rest in storage is critical. Adequate encryption of data at all times along with penetration testing is essential.
- Autonomous vehicles and drones are heavily dependent on automation and will present important cyber security concerns and require advance controls.
- Advances in, and maturing of, Artificial Intelligence use may result in increases in vulnerability to attacks. Defence

of facility systems and operations will need to include both software and hardware that rely on AI.
- Internet capable devices are projected to increase from an estimated 11 to 13 billion in 2013 to 200 billion in 2020. Various organizations are evaluating this area and need to develop additional standards. This includes the energy, manufacturing, healthcare, and transportation sectors.

Recent cyber security statistics from 2020, made by the European commission, highlight some important trends and vulnerabilities[79] :

- IoT attacks up by 600% in 2019;
- 350% increase in ransomware attacks annually;
- 65% of companies with > 500 employees have staff, who have never changed their password;
- 95% of cybersecurity breaches are due to human error;
- 31% of organizations have experienced cyber-attacks on operational infrastructure;
- 75% of the healthcare industry was infected with malware at least once;
- Approximately 50% of the cyber security exposure risk can be attributed to using multiple security vendors, equipment, and services.

Antivirus solutions are the most common and will defend against most types of malware. A hardware- or software-based firewall can provide an added layer of protection by preventing an unauthorized user from accessing a computer or network. Most modern operating systems, including Windows 10 and 11, come with a firewall program built in. Many security consultant, suggest businesses invest in three additional security measures along with those more surface-level tools.

- Data backup solution: This will ensure information compromised or lost during a breach can easily be recovered from an alternate location.
- Encryption software: To protect sensitive data, such

as employee records, client/customer information and financial statements, businesses should consider using encryption software.

- Two-step authentication or password-security software: Use these tools with internal programs to reduce the likelihood of password cracking.

As business begin considering different options and the security measures they would like to implement, it's generally a good idea to run a risk assessment, either by themselves or with the help of an outside firm. In addition to implementing software-based solutions, small businesses should adopt certain technological best practices and policies to shore up security vulnerabilities. If the company has an IT manager will play a significant role in all of these.

- Keep software up to date. Hackers are constantly scanning for security vulnerabilities and if the company allow these weaknesses to linger for too long, the company will significantly increase their chances of being targeted.
- Educate your employees. Teach your employees about the different ways cybercriminals can infiltrate your systems. Advise them on recognizing signs of a data breach, and educate them on how to stay safe while using the company's network.
- Implement formal security policies. Putting in place and enforcing security policies is essential to locking down your system. Protecting the network should be on everyone's mind since everyone who uses it can be a potential endpoint for attackers. Regularly hold meetings and seminars on the best cybersecurity practices, such as creating strong passwords, identifying and reporting suspicious emails, activating two-factor authentication, and not clicking on links and downloading attachments in emails.
- Practice the incident response plan. Despite the best efforts, there may come a time when the company falls

prey to a cyberattack. If that day comes, it's crucial the staff can handle the fallout. By drawing up a response plan, an attack can be quickly identified and quelled before doing too much damage.

Even though cybercrime is getting more sophisticated, so are the solutions. There are more than a dozen ways to secure business's devices and network and an increasing number of methods for secure file sharing. Even if the business is hacked, it can recover from a data breach. As threats continue to evolve, so will ways to combat them. By no means should the business be complacent or take a lax approach to protecting the business, but as the word implies, cybersecurity is designed to keep the business digitally secure.

One of the best tool mentioned multiple time in this paper that represent one of the best protection for the near future is the encryption. Encryption protects the data on computer and networks, reducing the chances that business will suffer data breaches. Full-disk encryption may be the best solution for small business. Business can obtain it through built-in programs or third-party vendors. For top encryption, business should back up their data and keep track of your encryption keys. Business should also create memorable but complex passwords and use WPA3 Wi-Fi and a VPN.

Encryption is a difficult concept to grasp, but it's a necessary part of protecting business's sensitive data. At a basic level, encryption is the process of scrambling text (called ciphertext) to render it unreadable to unauthorized users. Business owner can encrypt individual files, folders, volumes or entire disks within a computer, as well as USB flash drives and files stored in the cloud. The purpose of file and disk encryption is to protect data stored on a computer or network storage system. All organizations that collect personally identifiable information (PII) like names, birthdates, Social Security numbers and financial information must secure that data. An organization can be sued if a computer containing PII is stolen and the information is leaked or shared.

If a laptop is lost or stolen and the files or disk aren't encrypted, the thief can easily access the information, so it's a good practice to encrypt sensitive data, if not the entire hard drive. The thief doesn't even need to know the password to access the files; it's easy to boot a computer from a USB thumb drive and then access the disks within the computer. Disk encryption doesn't protect a computer entirely. A hacker can still access the computer over an insecure network connection, or a user can click a malicious link in an email and infect the computer with malware that steals usernames and passwords. Those types of attacks require additional security controls, like anti-malware software, firewalls and awareness training. However, encrypting a computer's files or the entire disk greatly reduces the risk of data theft. Encryption is a digital form of cryptography, which uses mathematical algorithms to scramble messages, leaving only individuals who possess the sender's cipher or key able to decode the message. There are two main methods of encryption: symmetric encryption, which involves securing data with a single private key, and asymmetric encryption, which uses a combination of multiple keys that are both public and private. The most common form of symmetric encryption is Advanced Encryption Standard (AES), which is the U.S. government standard for encryption. Data in hexadecimal form is scrambled multiple times and utilizes 128-bit, 192-bit, or 256-bit keys to unlock, the last being the strongest. Keys can be substituted with passwords that the owner create, making the password the only direct way to decrypt the data. This method is best for encrypting files and drives. The only weak spot is the password itself, which hackers may break if it's weak. They're unlikely to strong-arm their way into the data through encryption. Though 128-bit AES is a strong encryption key, most government regulations require the stronger 256-bit AES to meet certain standards. Asymmetric encryption is used for sending secured messages and other data between two individuals. On messaging platforms, such as most email services, all users have a public key and a private key. The public key acts as a type of address and method for the sender to encrypt their message. That message is further encrypted with the sender's private key. The receiver can then use the sender's public key to verify the message sender and then decrypt the message with their own private key. A hacker who intercepts the message will be unable to view its contents without the receiver's private key.

There are different types of encryption:

- Individual file and folder encryption: This method encrypts only the specific items that the owner tell it to. It is acceptable if relatively few business documents are stored on a computer, and it's better than no encryption at all.
- Volume encryption: This method creates a container of sorts that's fully encrypted. All files and folders created in or saved to that container are encrypted.
- Full-disk or whole-disk encryption: This is the most complete form of computer encryption. It's transparent to users and doesn't require them to save files to a special place on the disk. All files, folders and volumes are encrypted. The owner must provide an encryption passcode or have the computer read an encryption key (a random string of letters and numbers) from a USB device when powering on your computer. This action unlocks the files so you can use them normally.

The language of data encryption may make it seem impossible, but plenty of simple business encryption solutions exist. For starters, most computers come with built-in encryption programs, though you may have to manually enable some. Business can also install several third-party encryption programs for full-disk protection. Plenty of business anti-malware programs include encryption software, and some vendors sell stand-alone encryption tools too. Strong encryption is built into modern versions of the Windows and

OS X operating systems, and it's available for some Linux distributions as well.

Microsoft BitLocker is a disk encryption tool available on Windows 7, Windows 8.1 and Windows 10. It's designed to work with a Trusted Platform Module chip in business`s computer, which stores your disk encryption key. It's possible to enable BitLocker even without the chip, but a few settings must be configured within the operating system, which requires administrative privileges. BitLocker, Microsoft prompts to save a copy of your recovery key. This is an important step because is important to be able to recover the key to unlock the disk. Without the key, neither the owner nor anyone else cannot access the data. Is it possible to print the key or save it to a Microsoft account or a file. BitLocker also lets you require a personal identification number (PIN) at start up.

Apple FileVault provides encryption for computers running Mac OS X. When enabling encryption, FileVault prompts to store the disk encryption recovery key in an iCloud account, but is possible to choose to write it down instead.

For Linux, typically encrypt the disk during installation of the operating system, using a tool such as dm-crypt. However, third-party tools are also available for post-installation encryption.

Third party encryptions program are also very valuable and here some example:

- TrueCrypt used to be one of the most popular open-source disk encryption software programs, but its developers stopped maintaining it in 2014. Security experts are still torn on whether it's safe to use. To be on the safe side, stick with a product that's regularly tested and updated. These are a few open-source products that are well regarded:
- VeraCrypt is free software that runs on Windows, Mac OS X and Linux. It frequently gets the highest ratings from users and third-party testers.
- AxCrypt is an easy-to-use encryption program with

free and premium versions. It has a password manager and collaboration feature for sharing encrypted data with others.

- Gpg4win uses military-grade security to encrypt and digitally sign files and emails.
- Many anti-malware vendors – such as Symantec, Kaspersky, Sophos and ESET – include encryption in their security suites or sell it as a stand-alone product.
- USB drives should also be encrypted because when you copy files from an encrypted disk to a USB drive, the files can be automatically decrypted.

It's important to educate employees that once they send a file via email or copy it to a USB thumb drive, that data is no longer protected by that encryption, to avoid this there are some options for example to ensure files on a USB device are encrypted, it is possible to use software like Microsoft BitLocker To Go or open-source software, or purchase USB drives with built-in encryption, such as those from IronKey, SanDisk and Kanguru. Or when sending an email is important to password protect the file and send in a different email the password or communicate the password to the receiver in any other way.

According to the Ponemon Institute, the average cost of full-disk computer data encryption is 235 euros. This is quite affordable, given that data breaches can cost several orders of magnitude more to correct. Of course, encryption will prove more costly if you lose your key and access, so always keep track of the key.

Before enabling encryption on the business computer, back up your data files and create an image backup, which is a replica of all the contents of the disk. It is important also to ensure that it is in possession the operating system's installation media and create an emergency boot disk on removable media. Going forward, back up of computer files must be conducted regularly. An encrypted disk that crashes or becomes corrupt can result in files being lost forever. If the business is in possession of a current backup, the business can be up and running fairly quickly. When creating a passcode or PIN, it is recommended to use random numbers and letters, and memorize it. The longer and more complex it is, the better, but not so complex that could be forgotten. The business should consider putting two phrases together, like short verses from two songs for example. A written copy of your PIN or passcode and your encryption key should be kept in a safe place, in case it is forget. If it is enable a full-disk encryption and the owner forget the passcode, no one will be able to access the computer, including IT personnel and even data recovery services. If the business use Wi-Fi, should be used Wi-Fi Protected Access 3 (WPA3), which is a form of encryption for protecting wireless connections. Business should never use Wired Equivalent Privacy (WEP), which isn't safe under any circumstances. Even WPA2 was cracked in 2017, making it less safe than WPA3. Final step to have a full encrypted business needs to be installed a virtual private network (VPN) to access the office network from a laptop or other mobile device when working remotely. A VPN creates a secure tunnel over the internet, encrypting all data that you send and receive during that session. Computer encryption is only one part of a complete security plan for protecting computers and confidential data.

Other than the encryption something else that could be done is to safely store the data on the cloud, one of the best cloud service at the moment is provided by google. Google Drive enables backup and cloud collaboration for different file types on PCs and Macs. Drive File Stream is the backup solution for Google Workspace users, offering various controls and the ability to sync Microsoft Office files to a work or school account. Backup and Sync is the backup solution for consumers, with the ability to back up photos and documents on your computer's desktop. There's a simple method businesses can use to back up data on Google Drive. With Drive File Stream, Google's dedicated backup tool for enterprise users, it is possible to save different types of files stored on business's computers to Google's cloud backup system. Backup and Sync replaces the Google Drive application with a feature set that offers more detailed control over files and folders. Backup and Sync is designed to be an easier and faster way to upload documents, photos and other files to Google Drive and Google Photos. "It's a simpler, speedier and more reliable way to protect the files and photos that mean the most to you," Google announced in a statement. The company also claims Backup and Sync will keep files safe and organized on Google's servers, no longer "trapped" in the computer and other devices.

Drive File Stream is a Google Drive service that makes all cloud files available on the desktop without taking up space on the device. All-important files remain accessible without the need to visit Google Drive from the browser. To use Google Drive's File Stream, a designated Google Workspace administrator must enable it for the organization. It is possible to be able to specify that organization's users can allow Google Drive File Stream on their devices, and whether users can see the download links. One of Drive File Stream's key benefits is that administrators can enable real-time presence in Microsoft Office files. That means users can see if someone else is editing a shared Office file, preventing potential conflicts with the file version. Drive File Stream syncs hard drive files with what is backed up to the cloud. The service also makes it easy to back up and restore files to the machine if a new PC is starting over or need to wipe the hard drive.

To use Backup and Sync, install the Backup and Sync client on the computer, then select which folders in the computer needs to be backed up. Is possible also to back up and sync files from SD cards, USB devices, cameras, and mobile devices. After the initial setup, files in selected folders and data sources automatically upload to Google's servers and sync anytime a change happened. Backup and Sync creates a folder on the computer named Google Drive. Any files is in that folder automatically upload to and sync with My Drive folder on Google Drive and are accessible on all Drive-enabled devices or over the web.

Since Backup and Sync automatically uploads and syncs files

to the Google Drive account, is important to keep an eye on the storage space. Google gives all users 15GB of Drive storage for free. If the backing up files happened in large amount such as photos, videos, or entire computer, it is very likely that the business will need to consider a bigger space than 15GB.

Google changed how Google Drive and Photos work together in order to allow better control over the data between the two services. New photos and videos from Drive no longer automatically show in Photos, nor will they be automatically added to a Photos folder in Drive. However, existing items are not removed. Backup and Sync still allows to upload images and videos via High Quality or Original Quality. The former qualifies for free storage, while the latter counts against Drive quota.

Usually iCloud backup is the main method for backing up an iPhone, as it directly integrates with iOS, but it is possible to have all the data in Google Drive.

Get into the habit of regularly backing up the professional and personal files, including the following:

- Documents: Word documents, Excel spreadsheets, presentations and other files that the business need from day to day should be backed up. Even if a particular project has ended or don't need to regularly access the file, it's a good idea to save a copy just in case.
- Photos: Setting up automatic backup tools for photos ensures that are not lost.
- Media files: Songs, videos, movie files and other media should be backed up. While these are large and take up more room than documents and photos, the cloud should have plenty of space to hold them. If not, consider upgrading for more space.

Google recommends that Google Workspace users opt for Drive File Stream and recommends Backup and Sync for consumers. It is important to keep an eye on the evolving feature sets to ensure that business are taking full advantage of the services.

It's a necessary security control for organizations that handle confidential data, and it should be enabled on any device that could fall into the wrong hands.

# 3.4 HOW FAST THE SMALL AND MEDIUM BUSINESS NEED TO ADOPT THE RIGHT MEASURE OF CYBER SECURITY

When looking ahead at the future of cybersecurity, there's one major caveat to keep in mind: it could all change in a moment. Year after year, the industry changes. Cyber threats evolve, and the tools that defend against them mirror those changes, evolving in their own right to better defend increasingly complex networks. Unfortunately, 2022 began with major changes that had wide-reaching implications in the form of the Russia-Ukraine conflict[80]. After nearly two months of tension, Russian troops amassed on the Ukrainian border and invaded, leading to a widespread and prolonged conflict. The invasion was preceded by coordinated cyberattacks on 70 Ukrainian government websites, compromising 10 and defacing them with threatening messages; further activity targeting Ukrainian systems involved a wiper ware campaign in February of that year. It's hard to understate the severity and reach this conflict has had on the cybersecurity world at large. Businesses everywhere have had to look closely at their digital supply chains to ensure they're not dependent on partners or providers directly linked to or impacted by the conflict; what's more, it's widely accepted and expected that cyberattacks on Ukraine's allies and supporters will continue. The current status quo represents a dramatic shift in the cyber threat landscape, one whose full effects are still being understood. The existing cybercrime economy has been transformed by this conflict, and new threats continue to emerge. The Ukraine-Russia conflict will likely dominate numerous cybersecurity conversations in 2023 and beyond. The most apparent "normal" cybersecurity challenge revolves around remote work. With the hybrid office model here to stay, remote work (and the cyber risks it brings) will remain prevalent. Malicious actors look for vulnerable or misconfigured systems that connect to the internet, a much easier task after companies encouraged remote work due to pandemic concerns. "The biggest cybersecurity trend this year is the shift toward working at home," says Ernie Sherman, a Field Effect partner and the President of Fuelled Networks, a managed IT and security services provider that helps companies plan, manage, and align these services with their customers' business strategies. "The challenge this brings is that we can no longer assume that corporate resources are protected by perimeter security; we need to adopt a zero-trust model and assume that corporate resources and unsecured devices are sharing the same space and need to be secured accordingly." Cyber criminals have also been taking advantage of preoccupied or distracted remote workers and may continue to do so.

The last few years have been transformative for the cybersecurity industry including the bad guys. Rapid digital transformation brought about by changing office environments has given attackers a greater opportunity to target victims. Because of the growing cyber-crime-as-a-service (CaaS) economy, attackers can now rent or buy tools for an attack. This has freed up time to research and strategically target companies more likely to pay ransom or otherwise provide a better return on investment. With regulations like the General Data Privacy Regulation (GDPR), Personal Information Protection and Electronic Documents Act (PIPEDA), and California Consumer Privacy Act (CCPA) now in full force, data breach victims may face fines should confidential data become exposed. Attackers are exploiting this, adjusting ransom demands accordingly to make paying up more appealing than paying the regulatory penalty.

The past two decades have revealed a growing demand for information. Widespread adoption of social networking sites and applications has given users everywhere a way to access news and a wide variety of content, but they've also made it easier for malicious actors to exploit this need for information. These actors manipulate content, images, and videos to pursue their political agenda. Deep fakes, bots on social media, and other tactics are frequently used to spread false information or otherwise influence opinion. This is particularly evident in the immediate cyberwarfare efforts resulting from the Russia-Ukraine conflict as deep fakes and AI-enabled disinformation have been put to regular use for malicious purposes. The cybersecurity talent gap has long been a topic of discussion within the industry, and it's not going away any time soon. A recent report by (ISC) found that the global cybersecurity workforce grew by 11% in 2022, and the talent gap continued to grow by 26.2%. Demand vastly outpaces the supply of cybersecurity professionals as the need for talented staff rises throughout every sector. Cybersecurity has become a major concern for businesses everywhere. Labour market data company Emsi analysed cybersecurity job postings and found that for every 100 openings, there were fewer than 50 qualified candidates. Cybersecurity spending is unlikely to slow down any time soon. The International Data Corporation (IDC)forecasts that worldwide cybersecurity spending will reach 174.7 billion euros in 2024, with security services the largest and fastest-growing market segment. The rise in cyberattacks, especially ransomware, has fuelled the cyber insurance market. GlobalData, a leader in data and analytics, predicted that the industry would hit 8.92 billion euros in 2021 and more than double to 20.6 billion euros by 2025. Yet change has come to insurers offering coverage for cyberattacks[81].

The regulatory landscape continues to develop, even years after the introduction of the GDPR and CCPA. Both regulations have proven to be influential, shifting the conversation around data privacy away from harm prevention and towards the protection of rights. The European Union, United States Data Privacy Framework, introduced in late 2022, creates further controls and protections for individual data rights, such as transfer of data between the two regions and the surveillance policies of various intelligence agencies. The EU–U.S. Data Privacy Framework is still under review by the European Commission. In the United States, four additional states are following California's lead with the CCPA and introducing state-level legislation of their own, due to take effect in 2023, Colorado, Connecticut, Virginia, and Utah, and 20 states have inactive data privacy regulations that could be revived. Likewise, numerous Canadian provinces have introduced additional privacy legislation, such as Quebec's Bill 64. This legislation, along with proposed laws in British Columbia, Alberta, and Ontario, is giving authorities greater power to address data breaches and privacy concerns. These laws create further responsibilities for organizations headquartered or handling data within the province that go beyond existing PIPEDA controls.

Once upon a time, simply having a cyber insurance policy in place was more than enough, and insurers could be counted on to simply cover the costs of an attack without question. Yet amidst the global coronavirus pandemic and the resulting surge of cyberattacks, insurers became far more stringent, suddenly leery of simply footing the bill for every attack "gone are the five-question applications," say KPMG analysts[82]. Premium rates increased the board, contributing to the growth of the industry[83]; in 2021, the estimated value of the cyber insurance market was US $12.83 billion—and by 2029, it is expected this will increase to $63.62 billion. However, this growth came at a price: small and mid-sized businesses (SMBs), already forced to stretch every dollar, were stuck with the bill. 2023 brings with it good news, though. After this unsettled period, the market looks set to stabilize, albeit with the caveat that it's not returning to pre-pandemic accessibility. Underwriters everywhere will be far more judicious and demanding when offering coverage, expecting to see some degree of cybersecurity maturity from their clients. Businesses looking to access the protections offered by a cyber insurance plan should expect greater scrutiny of their cybersecurity program, including some detection and response capabilities and evidence of ongoing education and awareness efforts.

Artificial intelligence (AI) has become a buzzword in industries everywhere, and cybersecurity is no exception. We've all seen the transformative potential of these tools, as well as the outlandish promises and claims that AI will solve all our problems. The truth of things is that most so-called AI is, in fact, a machine learning system that has been trained to identify specific patterns. The future of AI in cybersecurity is not quite as magical as slick marketing and sales speak would have you think. While automation is necessary to handle the sheer volume of threat data modern solutions ingest, human intelligence is just as important. All that data needs to be interpreted to spot emerging threats and stop attacks in their tracks. Looking ahead into 2023 and beyond, expect to see renewed interest in applying so-called AI or machine learning to reduce the amount of manual effort needed to parse the vast quantities of alert data generated by cybersecurity tech stacks.

There are a growing number of trends and potential threats that businesses should continue to keep an eye on, regardless of size or industry[84].

- The cybercrime-as-a-service economy puts

the accumulated knowledge and tools of thousands, if not millions, of hackers and cyber criminals at the fingertips of an individual attacker. This makes it easy for inexperienced hackers to rapidly stage complex attacks. CaaS marketplaces continue to operate despite several major takedowns by law enforcement agencies as malicious actors adapt their tactics and techniques to stay under the radar.

- Malware attacks are increasingly automated, continuing a recent trend that has forced the cybersecurity industry to catch up. Security experts are no longer dealing with lone hackers testing their skills with hard-to-execute attacks. Now, hackers can use a machine to automate cybercrime activities, letting them execute thousands of attacks a day. Ransomware is so common that only the largest attacks seem to garner media attention.

- A greater number of malware variants now contain polymorphic characteristics, which means they constantly change their identifiable features to better hide from security teams and common detection techniques. Many CaaS offerings contain some element of code that can mutate so it can remain hidden.

- As companies continue to ramp up their efforts and adopt digital technologies, many turn to third parties, outsourcing some IT and security support needs. As we've discussed before, reliance on third parties increases cybersecurity risks, especially for companies that do not have a strategy in place for managing these risks.

- The one constant in cybersecurity is the human element. As Matt Holland, Field Effect's co-founder, CEO, and CTO once commented, "The human element is often the problem the large majority of the time, be it clicking on a link or misconfiguring a network, and that is something I think goes understated." Humans are always present in technology at some point, whether developing, configuring, or simply using it, and humans make mistakes. Education, training, and vigilance are necessary to help reduce the likelihood of a mistake having a serious impact.

Looking past 2023, there are a few threats and trends that may make up the future of cybersecurity[85]:

- In the next five years, the use of IoT technology will increase as more people use it in their day-to-day lives. According to data from IoT Analytics, there were 10 billion connected devices in 2019 and we could see that triple to 30.9 billion by 2025. For added context, 2019 was also the year that the number of IoT connections outpaced that of non-IoT. Despite connecting to networks and other devices that access highly sensitive information, IoT devices continue to have relatively weak security controls. Many businesses already struggle to provide the added defence measures that will keep these devices (and everything they're connected to) secure.

- In five years, internet communications will likely become more secure, especially with the potential rise of quantum networks which will make network-based threats less relevant. One ongoing challenge is that of human error. Intentionally or not, employees will still enable data loss and attackers will still rely on social engineering tricks such as phishing and business email compromise.

- Payment modernization means that financial transactions may become almost entirely digital, requiring support from various platforms and methods. These platforms will likely be less centralized, and regulations will take time to catch up. This will expand the threat surface for financial institutions and tool, resulting in more fraud-oriented security solutions focused on digital currencies, the blockchain, and real-time payment security.

- Despite a growing number of countries prioritizing cybersecurity, a lack of attributable data for criminal acts conducted online will make it hard for law enforcement to prosecute cyber criminals. A shortage of cybersecurity professionals will also contribute, making it harder to proactively find cyber threats.

For one, a greater focus on prevention and preparedness will be vital. Response planning for a security incident or data breach is necessary. Incident preparedness and response playbooks will likely become more commonplace. Employee training at every level will mitigate the role of human error.

For years, threat actors have been mirroring technological changes, tweaking and refining their attack tactics to achieve greater success. We saw this first-hand years ago with the flurry of pandemic-themed phishing scams, assaults on improperly configured cloud apps, and more. As someone with a pivotal role in securing private company data and systems, you know how critical it is to stay on top of new and emerging risks. As companies have adjusted to the modern hybrid work environment, we witnessed a stark increase in the adoption of remote access tools, video conferencing apps, and cloud-based services. Hackers may focus their attacks on:

- Remote desktop apps
- Misconfigured web-based services
- Legacy operating systems
- Unpatched internet–facing applications
- Outdated browsers

Also see a focus on server less attacks as organizations continue adopting the cloud-service model. To stay safe, business should remind employees that they are a target and can defend themselves by remaining vigilant and following cybersecurity best practices, such as:

- Patching software regularly
- Using strong passwords
- Backing up data regularly

Another top cyber threat in 2023 is the flourishing CaaS

economy. New research found that off-the-shelf malware has never been easier to find or cheaper to buy, and almost anyone can find hundreds of illegal marketplaces in mere seconds. Threat actors will continue participating in criminal online marketplaces, renting and selling items such as:

- Phishing and exploit kits to gain initial access to victim systems
- Stolen account credentials to impersonate a legitimate user
- Databases of confidential personal and corporate information
- Ransomware services and malware to encrypt and extort victims
- Infrastructure to run the malware

Despite extensive efforts by law enforcement to take down these online marketplaces, they still exist. This ability to buy and rent malware means anyone, even those with little or no hacking skills, can become a cybercriminal. The total number of attacks increase as threat actors capitalize on a highly scalable income stream and the fact that they no longer need a technical skillset to hack systems. They can simply buy or rent the tools to carry out their attack, and at a low price too. Most companies have realized the importance of properly backing up data in case they're the victim of a ransomware attack. But there's a new extortion technique that renders these efforts insufficient. Attackers start by doing their homework, researching the target's assets and financials, and use this intel to set a ransom fee. Then, instead of encrypting the data and offering a decryption key in exchange for money, they threaten to release sensitive information publicly if the victim doesn't pay. They coerce the target into paying by threatening to cause a data breach, a technique that exploits new privacy regulations that penalize companies for not properly securing private data. Attackers depend on the fact that their ransom may cost less than the penalties, fines, and reputation damage the company may face if they choose not to pay. Internet of Things (IoT) devices, such as smart security cameras and thermostats, are quickly becoming a valuable target for attackers. IoT devices connect to networks, cloud apps, and other technologies, and offer endless productivity benefits for businesses and individuals alike. Unfortunately, these devices are often connected to valuable company assets but are rarely built with security in mind, making them a weak link in your company's cyber strategy. And while IoT manufacturers have started to focus more on incorporating security controls, many still prioritize functionality and affordability. Phishing continues to be one of the easiest, cheapest, and most popular cyberattack methods, and our team expects it will remain a top cyber threat in 2023 and beyond. But to ensure success and a higher return on investment, attackers may become more selective while choosing their victim. This is spear-phishing. Thanks in part to the CaaS economy and phishing-as-a-service offerings, attackers can spend less time developing tools and more time researching their targets. They may form their attacks using personal information gained from social media accounts and company websites to create more convincing, and therefore successful, spear phishing campaigns. Attackers may target specific groups, such as:

- Online retailers, as they may operate on unsecured e-commerce platforms
- Virtual education platforms, due to the increasing number of users
- Healthcare institutions, as they collect a lot of sensitive data and, due to the critical nature of their business, may be more likely to pay a ransom

Living off the land (LOTL) attacks remain a top cyber threat. Despite being mainstream for many years already, LOTL attacks often go undetected for long periods. These attacks make use of tools already installed on targeted computers, instead of uploading and executing custom malware, for example, a feature that makes them challenging to defend against. Because they don't generate any new files, attackers can fly under the radar of many security tools and cause significant amounts of damage. Consider this as you add or swap out security solutions this year. Covalence is one example of a cybersecurity platform intelligent enough to spot a wide range of threats and vulnerabilities, including discreet LOTL attacks.

Cybersecurity is a constantly evolving field. As new threats emerge, new security solutions are needed to defend against them.

# 3.5 CONCLUSION

Large business are already implanting new measure but they still need to conduct a security vulnerability assessment and implement security measures that meet risk-based performance standards (RBPS), which cover such areas as perimeter security, access control, personnel authorization and cyber security. Emphasizing the need for:

- Appointment of a cyber security officer
- Managing access control to company computer systems (i.e., controls on what devices employees, vendors, and customers can connect to the system)
- Effective password management
- Setting appropriate levels of system access for each user
- Effective and recurring training and awareness
- System monitoring and incident management
- Life cycle and configuration management
- Layered computer security

Should also be developed a program to provide coordination and outreach in the protection of cyber components of critical infrastructure. Also should be developed Cybersecurity Framework Function Areas and sector-specific guidance for all six critical infrastructure sectors, for both private and public: Chemical, Commercial Facilities, Critical Manufacturing, Dams, Emergency Services, and Nuclear.

A security program in general needs to outline for development and implementation of:

- Identify – establish the organizational structure to manage cyber security risk to systems, assets, data, and

capabilities
- Protect – create safeguards to ensure delivery of critical infrastructure services
- Detect – perform activities to identify the occurrence of a cyber security event
- Respond – develop actions in the event of a detected cyber security event
- Recover – implement activities that maintain plans and enhance resilience and restore impaired company capabilities or services

Staying informed, sharing information and acting on general industry cyber vulnerabilities as they are discovered is another key component of a prevention program. Sharing cyber vulnerability information must take into account the following:
- Whether the vulnerability has been publicly disclosed
- Severity of vulnerability
- Potential impact to critical infrastructure
- Possible threat to public health and safety
- Immediate mitigation actions available
- Vendor/supplier responsiveness
- Feasibility of creating an upgrade or patch
- Time required for technology users to obtain, test and implement a patch

These risk factors should be embraced by industry as they attempt to quantify their own company's exposure.

It is important to remember that cyber security, like all security, is a process, not a product. Cyber security must be an on-going action by all employees and contractors of a company/ entity. Many companies have internal IT security departments, training, and vendor assisted programs to raise awareness of the potential types of cyberattacks and to provide clear guidance on reporting suspicious activity. Further, there are now cyber security journals, training programs, college degree programs, and government information available as resources that can help industry stay current with trends and threats. A literature search reveals a limited number of readily available cyber security sample programs, likely due to the sensitivity of the subject matter. However, some public entities and organizations have developed templates and/or guidance for their membership.

A Security program should incorporates existing consensus-based standards to:

- Identify existing cyber security standards, guidelines, frameworks, and best practices that will increase the security of critical infrastructure
- Specify high-priority gaps where new or revised standards are needed
- Collaboratively develop action plans to close these cyber gaps.

Cyber resilience increase awareness of exposures, and provide a framework for improving critical infrastructure cyber security. This public-private partnership provides existing resources to assist with implementation of Cyber Security Framework as part of a comprehensive enterprise risk management program. Companies should take care to verify the accuracy of cyber security related information and any Internet provided guidance. It is best to have direct interaction with vendors, suppliers and outside consultants to better evaluate capabilities and experience.

Small business instead might not see the immediate need to act on their cyber security protection, as they don`t feel as exposed as the large business, it was mention in this paper multiple times that the vulnerability of the large business is much greater compared to the small and medium as they might be a target of different types of cyberattacks, involving even political goals. So far the legislation doesn`t force small and medium business to take action to protect in protecting themselves against cyberattacks, exception is given to the GDPR as mention before involved everyone in contact with any type of data, in which should be raised but the government more awareness as many owners are not even aware of the existence of this European law. For an independent evaluation, it is highly recommended that companies retain a qualified cyber security consulting firm with relevant industry experience prior to developing and implementing a new cyber security program. These firms are more likely to be able to identify vulnerabilities and emerging threats than in-house efforts. In addition to a plan, companies need to develop and implement awareness training on company policies and procedures as these are developed. Refresher training and system tests/response (i.e. fake phishing drills, etc.) are warranted to reinforce computer security concepts. Systems also need to be in place to assess the effectiveness of plans and training. An attitude of "it can't happen to us" can be very detrimental to a company, its employees, and stakeholders. All industries and businesses must continue to be highly cognizant of the detrimental and potentially devastating effects a cyberattack can have on an organization. This includes catastrophic environmental impacts, fires, explosions and other consequences that are possible from a single cyberattack and can result in business interruption, reputational impacts, significant financial loss, and regulatory actions/enforcement.

To close this paper every single type of enterprise should build a cybersecurity culture to protect their business and have in this way reliance in case something happen. The best way to do this is always to anticipate, recognise and recover. Anticipating by creating all possible measure to prevent incidents and accidents to happen, recognising by checking their systems constantly to spot possible attacks and recovering by minimizing the damage when something happen. To summarize a At a minimum, a company's cyber security program should include:

- Program management
- Planning
- Awareness training/procedures training/notification

training
- Configuration management
- Firewalls
- Content filtering
- Intrusion prevention systems
- Patch management systems
- Penetration testing and security auditing
- Quick response/quick response team
- Security assessment
- Risk assessment
- Physical protection of assets and personnel
- Contingency planning
- Security system management/oversight programs
- Connectivity (protection of businesses, systems, and control systems with the Internet.)
- Vulnerability assessment
- Implement action plan

To fight or minimize potentially negative outcomes, each business needs to take cyber security seriously and develop and implement robust cyber security measures. This should include initial and periodic vulnerability assessments, awareness training and on-going prevention and monitoring programs. Much like any safety or security program, a penny of prevention may be worth millions in a cure.

Cybersecurity still needs to find its proper place within the traditional notion of security. While security is a concern as ancient as humanity, cybersecurity is a relatively recent concept that is still in need of assessment and elaboration. Especially in the world of small and medium size business, the hope is that the national`s government and all active business owners start to structure their business in the direction of a more secure cyber world.

# REFERENCES AND BIBLIOGRAPHY

[1] Wong, J.C. The Cambridge Analytica scandal changed the world – but it didn't change Facebook. Available in: https://www.theguardian.com/technology/2019/mar/17/the-cambridge-analytica-scandal-changed-the-world-but-it-didnt-change-facebook [18 March 2019].

[2] Coburn, T. What Is a Cyberattack?. Available in: https://www.cisco.com/c/en/us/products/security/common-cyberattacks.html#~types-of-cyber-attacks [30 April 2016].

[3] Coburn, T. What Is a Cyberattack?. Available in: https://www.cisco.com/c/en/us/products/security/common-cyberattacks.html#~types-of-cyber-attacks [30 April 2016].

[4] Wong, J.C. The Cambridge Analytica scandal changed the world – but it didn't change Facebook. Available in: https://www.theguardian.com/technology/2019/mar/17/the-cambridge-analytica-scandal-changed-the-world-but-it-didnt-change-facebook [18 March 2019].

[5] Confessore, N. Cambridge Analytica and Facebook: The Scandal and the Fallout So Far. Available in: https://www.nytimes.com/2018/04/04/us/politics/cambridge-analytica-scandal-fallout.html [4 April 2018].

[6] Zeshan , N. Top 10 Cybersecurity Tips to Stay Protected. Available in: https://www.knowledgehut.com/blog/security/cyber-security-tips [30 January 2023]

[7] Zeshan , N. Top 10 Cybersecurity Tips to Stay Protected. Available in: https://www.knowledgehut.com/blog/security/cyber-security-tips [30 January 2023]

[8] Kotha, A. How Large Enterprises Can Proactively Secure Themselves Against Cybersecurity Attacks. Available in: https://www.forbes.com/sites/forbestechcouncil/2023/02/09/how-large-enterprises-can-proactively-secure-themselves-against-cybersecurity-attacks/?sh=6d725812130d [30 January 2023]

[9] Pernik P. Wojtkowiak J. Verschoor-Kirss A. (2016). National Cyber Security Organisation: UNITED STATES. CCDCOE

[10] Chin, K. Biggest Data Breaches in US History. Available in: https://www.upguard.com/blog/biggest-data-breaches-us [28 March 2023]

[11] Communication bureau office. Cybersecurity for Small Businesses. Available in: https://www.fcc.gov/communications-business-opportunities/cybersecurity-small-businesses

[12] Checkpoint auditor. Biggest Data Breaches in US History. Available in: https://www.checkpoint.com/cyber-hub/cyber-security/what-is-cyber-attack/

[13] Banafa, A. The Future of Cybersecurity: Predictions and Trends. Available in: https://www.bbvaopenmind.com/en/technology/digital-world/future-of-cybersecurity-predictions-trends/ [03 April 2023].

[14] Pernik P. Wojtkowiak J. Verschoor-Kirss A. (2016). National Cyber Security Organisation: UNITED STATES. CCDCOE

[15] Clayton, M. Assessing Cybersecurity Regulations. Available in: https://obamawhitehouse.archives.gov/blog/2014/05/22/assessing-cybersecurity-regulations [22 May 2022].

[16] Pernik P. Wojtkowiak J. Verschoor-Kirss A. (2016). National Cyber Security Organisation: UNITED STATES. CCDCOE

[17] Oxley act. (2002). https://www.govinfo.gov/content/pkg/COMPS-1883/pdf/COMPS-1883.pdf

[18] Driver's Privacy Protection Act. (1994). https://dmv.ny.gov/forms/mv15dppa.pdf

[19] Children's Online Privacy Protection Act. (1998). http://euro.ecom.cmu.edu/program/law/08-732/Regulatory/coppa.pdf

[20] Video Privacy Protection Act. (2012). https://www.govinfo.gov/content/pkg/COMPS-10163/pdf/COMPS-10163.pdf

[21] Shield act. (2020). https://www.cov.com/-/media/files/corporate/publications/2020/03/new-york-shield-act-data-security-requirements-become-effective.pdf

[22] The Illinois Biometric Information Privacy Act. (1998). https://www.ilga.gov/legislation/ilcs/ilcs3.asp?ActID=3004&ChapterID=57

[23] California Privacy Rights Act .(2020). https://www.weil.com/-/media/the-california-privacy-rights-act-of-2020-may-2021.pdf

[24] Consumer Data Protection Act. (2021). https://lis.virginia.gov/cgi-bin/legp604.exe?212+ful+CHAP0036+pdf

[25] Colorado Privacy Act. (2021). https://leg.colorado.gov/sites/default/files/2021a_190_signed.pdf

[26] Utah Consumer Privacy Act. (2022). https://le.utah.gov/~2022/bills/sbillenr/SB0227.pdf

[27] Gramm Leach Bliley Act. (1999). https://www.govinfo.gov/content/pkg/PLAW-106publ102/pdf/PLAW-106publ102.pdf

[28] Fair Credit Reporting Act. (2018). https://www.ftc.gov/system/files/

documents/statutes/fair-credit-reporting-act/545a_fair-credit-reporting-act-0918.pdf

[29] Fair and Accurate Credit Transactions Act. (2023). https://www.congress.gov/108/plaws/publ159/PLAW-108publ159.pdf

[30] Payment Card Industry Data Security Standard. (2018). https://www.commerce.uwo.ca/pdf/PCI_DSS_v3-2-1.pdf

[31] Health Information Portability and Accountability Act. (1996). https://www.govinfo.gov/app/details/PLAW-104publ191

[32] Telephone Consumer Protection Act. (2003). https://www.fcc.gov/sites/default/files/tcpa-rules.pdf

[33] Cyber security act. (2019). https://eur-lex.europa.eu/legal-content/EN/ALL/?uri=CELEX%3A32019R0881

[34] National Response Plan: Cyber Incident Annex', Federal Emergency Management Agency, 2004. http://www.fema.gov/media-library-data/20130726-1825-25045- 8307/cyber_incident_annex_2004.pdf .

[35] Moteff, John D., 'Critical Infrastructures: Background, Policy, and Implementation', Congressional Research Service, 2014 .

[36] Selyukh, Alina, 'U.S. to Offer Companies Broad Standards to Improve Cybersecurity,' Reuters, 2014, http://www.reuters.com/article/2014/02/12/us-usa-cybersecurity-standardsidUSBREA1B0AL20140212.

[37] Chamber of Commerce, 2014 Cybersecurity Education & Framework Awareness Campaign. Improving Today. Protecting Tomorrow, https://www.uschamber.com/programs/nationalsecurity-emergency-preparedness/2015-cybersecurity-campaign/education-awareness

[38] European union agency for cybersecurity. https://www.enisa.europa.eu/

[39] Nis directive. https://www.enisa.europa.eu/topics/cybersecurity-policy/nis-directive-new

[40] Nis2 directive. https://eur-lex.europa.eu/eli/dir/2022/2555

[41] European Cyber Security Organization. https://ecs-org.eu/

[42] Computer Security Incident Response Teams. https://www.csirt.gov.it/

[43] Computer Emergency Response Teams. https://european-union.europa.eu/institutions-law-budget/institutions-and-bodies/search-all-eu-institutions-and-bodies/computer-emergency-response-team-eu-institutions-bodies-and-agencies-cert-eu_en#:~:text=CERT%2DEU%20comprises%20a%20team,related%20to%20unclassified%20ICT%20infrastructure.

[44] Joint Research Center. https://joint-research-centre.ec.europa.eu/index_en

[45] General Data Protection Regulation. (2016). https://eur-lex.europa.eu/legal-content/EN/TXT/PDF/?uri=CELEX:32016R0679

[46] Checkpoint. How To Develop a Cyber Security Strategy. Available in: https://www.checkpoint.com/cyber-hub/cyber-security/what-is-cybersecurity/how-to-develop-a-cyber-security-strategy/#:~:text=An%20effective%20cybersecurity

%20strategy%20focuses,an%20attack%20to%20the%20organization.

[47] European Cyber Crises Liaison Organisation Network. https:// digital-strategy.ec.europa.eu/en/news/eu-countries-test-their-ability-cooperate-event-cyber-attacks

[48] Nis directive. https://eur-lex.europa.eu/legal-content/EN/ALL/?uri=CELEX %3A32016L1148

[49] Nis directive. https://eur-lex.europa.eu/legal-content/EN/ALL/?uri=CELEX %3A32016L1148

[50] Cyber security act. (2019). https://eur-lex.europa.eu/legal-content/EN/ALL/? uri=CELEX%3A32019R0881 Art 1.1

[51] Cyber security act. (2019). https://eur-lex.europa.eu/legal-content/EN/ALL/? uri=CELEX%3A32019R0881 Art 1.1

[52] Cyber security act. (2019). https://eur-lex.europa.eu/legal-content/EN/ALL/? uri=CELEX%3A32019R0881 Art 2.1

[53] Cyber security act. (2019). https://eur-lex.europa.eu/legal-content/EN/ALL/? uri=CELEX%3A32019R0881 Art 2.8

[54] Charter of Fundamental Rights https://www.europarl.europa.eu/charter/pdf/ text_en.pdf

[55] TFEU https://eur-lex.europa.eu/LexUriServ/LexUriServ.do? uri=CELEX:12012E/TXT:en:PDF Art114

[56] TFEU https://eur-lex.europa.eu/LexUriServ/LexUriServ.do? uri=CELEX:12012E/TXT:en:PDF Art 100

[57] TFEU https://eur-lex.europa.eu/LexUriServ/LexUriServ.do? uri=CELEX:12012E/TXT:en:PDF Art 114

[58] Cyber security act. (2019). https://eur-lex.europa.eu/legal-content/EN/ALL/? uri=CELEX%3A32019R0881 Art 1.2

[59] Security Intelligence Department. https://www.sicurezzanazionale.gov.it/ sisr.nsf/english.html

[60] Italian cyber security action plan. https://www.sicurezzanazionale.gov.it/ sisr.nsf/wp-content/uploads/2019/05/Italian-cybersecurity-action-plan-2017.pdf

[61] 2019/881. (2019) https://eur-lex.europa.eu/legal-content/IT/TXT/PDF/? uri=CELEX:32019R0881&from=PT

[62] Decree 82. (2021) https://eur-lex.europa.eu/legal-content/IT/TXT/PDF/? uri=CELEX:32019R0881&from=PT

[63] Decree 82. (2021) https://eur-lex.europa.eu/legal-content/IT/TXT/PDF/? uri=CELEX:32019R0881&from=PT

[64] Decree 82. (2021) https://eur-lex.europa.eu/legal-content/IT/TXT/PDF/? uri=CELEX:32019R0881&from=PT Art1

[65] Decree 82. (2021) https://eur-lex.europa.eu/legal-content/IT/TXT/PDF/? uri=CELEX:32019R0881&from=PT Art 2

[66] Decree 82. (2021) https://eur-lex.europa.eu/legal-content/IT/TXT/PDF/?

uri=CELEX:32019R0881&from=PT Art 3

[67] Decree 82. (2021) https://eur-lex.europa.eu/legal-content/IT/TXT/PDF/?uri=CELEX:32019R0881&from=PT Art 4

[68] Decree 82. (2021) https://eur-lex.europa.eu/legal-content/IT/TXT/PDF/?uri=CELEX:32019R0881&from=PT Art 5

[69] Field Effect. Top cyber threats to watch for in 2023. Available in: https://obamawhitehouse.archives.gov/blog/2014/05/22/assessing-cybersecurity-regulations [06 March 2023].

[70] Schulze, M. Cyber Operations in Russia's War against Ukraine. Available in: https://www.swp-berlin.org/10.18449/2023C23/ [17 April 2023].

[71] Costa Rica ransomware attack. Available in: https://cyberlaw.ccdcoe.org/wiki/Costa_Rica_ransomware_attack_(2022) [31 may 2022].

[72] FBI IC3 Releases 2022 Internet Crime Report. Available in: https://octillolaw.com/insights/fbi-ic3-releases-2022-internet-crime-report/#:~:text=In%202022%2C%20the%20IC3%20received,only%20351%2C937%20complaints%20in%20total. [23 March 2023].

[73] Filipkowski, B. What is the future of cybersecurity? Available in: https://fieldeffect.com/blog/what-is-the-future-of-cyber-security [24 March 2023].

[74] Cybint. 15 Alarming Cyber Security Facts and Stats. Available on: https://www.cybintsolutions.com/cyber-security-facts-stats/( August 2022)

[75] FMGlobal/Advisen. New Technology, New Risk: Cyber Concerns For Industrial Control Systems. Available on: https://www.advisenltd.com/wp-content/uploads/2017/07/cyber-concerns-for-industrial-control-systems-paper-2017-07-26.pdf

[76] Il Messagero 23rd of February 2023

[77] Rural Cooperative Cybersecurity Capabilities. Available on: https://www.cooperative.com/programs-services/bts/rc3/Pages/default.aspx

[78] (Guide To Developing A Cyber Security And Risk Mitigation Plan Template; National RuralElectricCooperative;https://www.smartgrid.gov/files/CyberSecurityGuideforanElectricCooperativeV11-21.pdf)

[79] Environmental risks: cyber security and critical industries. Solutions For Security By Design;VDMAMining;https://mining.vdma.org/documents/105698/30836548/BoG%20VDMA%202019%20full%20issue_1554296211901.pdf/a943fd43-efb5-3272-3583-31add9895d9e.

[80] Russia- ukraine

[81] stats

[82] kpmg

[83] Grwth of industry

[84] Potential threats

[85] Future of cybersecurity

# EPILOGUE

As we conclude this journey through the realm of cybersecurity for small and medium businesses, it's important to remember that the digital landscape is constantly evolving. New threats emerge, vulnerabilities are discovered, and technologies advance at an astonishing pace.

Therefore, cybersecurity is not a one-time endeavor but rather an ongoing journey. It requires vigilance, adaptability, and a commitment to continuous learning. By staying informed about the latest threats and trends, regularly updating security measures, and fostering a culture of cybersecurity awareness within your organization, you can significantly enhance your resilience against cyberattacks.

Remember, cybersecurity is not just a technical issue; it's a strategic imperative. By investing in cybersecurity, you're safeguarding your business's reputation, protecting your customers' trust, and preserving your hard-earned success. Let's embrace the challenges and opportunities of the digital age, and together, build a more secure and resilient future.

www.ingramcontent.com/pod-product-compliance
Lightning Source LLC
LaVergne TN
LVHW051336050326
832903LV00031B/3570